"Whatever venture or calling you live, relationships are the lifeblood. If you have ever desired to engage others in an exciting endeavor or longed to experience rich, meaningful community, Tim Muehlhoff's insights are worth your time. If you have any desire to make a difference in this world, you must understand how to steward the power of words. There are insights here worth your time!"

Greg Lillestrand, US director, Cru

"Over the years, Tim Muehlhoff's thoughts and guidance on personal communication have helped me grow as a person and as a leader. In *I Beg to Differ*, he once again provides me with strategies I can immediately apply to what I do every day, in business and in my personal life."

Jon Basalone, executive vice president, marketing and merchandising, Trader Joe's Company

"This is a deeply wise book. In it, Tim Muehlhoff offers hope, but not just hope; he also provides practical tools to help us communicate about differences in ways that foster growth more than division. Illustrating the book are powerful examples that are illuminated by Muehlhoff's seamless blending of insights from communication research and lessons from the Scriptures. The result is a book that resonates powerfully with our lives and invites us to become better versions of ourselves."

Julia T. Wood, Lineberger Distinguished Professor of Humanities, Emerita, University of North Carolina at Chapel Hill

"Conflict can be an indicator light of a relationship trending toward intimacy. Because of this, if we want to experience the joys of long-term, authentic relationships, we have to learn how to navigate conflict well. My friend Tim Muehlhoff gives us a strategy and practical tools to help guide us in having those sometimes unpleasant but necessary encounters."

Bryan Loritts, lead pastor, Fellowship Memphis

"Tim Muehlhoff provides winsome strategies for moving positively through difficult relational scenarios by the power of dialogue. His holistic approach weds insightful communication principles with the foundational issues of credibility, confidence and spiritual enablement, offering informed wisdom to readers dealing with a broad swath of communication impasses. The payoff is genuine hope that peaceful resolutions are possible, even in our most troublesome and painful conversations, as we walk on a path of truth and love."

Dr. Jon and Pam Lunde, Talbot School of Theology

"For more than twenty years, I have benefited both personally and professionally from Tim's wisdom and coaching. He is a masterful communicator, and the principals contained in his most recent book are stunning. I can't say that I am looking forward to the next difficult conversation that I will have to have with a family member or friend, but I am confident that the timeless and proven principles contained in *I Beg to Differ* will help me communicate with integrity and clarity."

Chris Willard, director of generosity initiatives and premium service, Leadership Network, and coauthor of *Contagious Generosity*

"I head up a graduate program in Christian apologetics and I can't think of a better book to read if you want to engage others with the 'humility and respect' that the apostle writes about in 1 Peter 3:15. But understand, this book is for everybody: evangelists, pastors, spouses, friends, bosses, employees—anyone who needs to communicate with charity, confidence and clarity. Tim Muehlhoff has written yet another incredibly helpful book that really needs to be read far and wide."

Craig J. Hazen, founder and director of the Christian Apologetics Program at Biola University and author of *Five Sacred Crossings*

"One doesn't have to look far to find myriad examples of incivility—from political commentators who cut off and ridicule their guests to boardrooms to church and faculty meetings to the dinner table. I can think of no one better than Tim Muehlhoff to provide insight and practical wisdom on how to navigate difficult conversations with grace and truth. Tim doesn't just apply his considerable scholarly expertise and biblical knowledge to the subject; he lives what he writes."

Carol Taylor, president, Evangel University

"Having worked in college ministry for over twenty years, we are always looking for resources to help people engage those with differing views on campus. With Tim Muehlhoff's help, even difficult conversations can foster understanding instead of driving a wedge."

Bob and Jill Fuhs, Cru staff, Los Angeles and Orange County

"Tim has the gift of taking profound insights based on solid scholarship and Scripture and making them easily understandable and practical. He exudes integrity in his own life and communication. I plan to study and apply the principles in this book!"

Roger Hershey, national speaker, Cru, and author of *The Finishers*

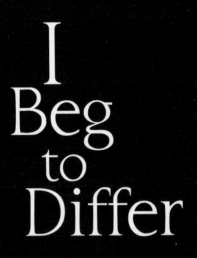

I Beg to Differ

NAVIGATING DIFFICULT
CONVERSATIONS WITH
TRUTH AND LOVE

TIM MUEHLHOFF

IVP Books

An imprint of InterVarsity Press
Downers Grove, Illinois

InterVarsity Press
P.O. Box 1400, Downers Grove, IL 60515-1426
World Wide Web: www.ivpress.com
Email: email@ivpress.com

InterVarsity Press® is the book-publishing division of InterVarsity Christian Fellowship/USA®, a movement of students and faculty active on campus at hundreds of universities, colleges and schools of nursing in the United States of America, and a member movement of the International Fellowship of Evangelical Students. For information about local and regional activities, write Public Relations Dept., InterVarsity Christian Fellowship/USA, 6400 Schroeder Rd., P.O. Box 7895, Madison, WI 53707-7895, or visit the IVCF website at www.intervarsity.org.

All Scripture quotations, unless otherwise indicated, are taken from THE HOLY BIBLE, NEW INTERNATIONAL VERSION®, NIV® Copyright © 1973, 1978, 1984, 2011 by Biblica, Inc.™ Used by permission. All rights reserved worldwide.

While all stories in this book are true, some names and identifying information in this book have been changed to protect the privacy of the individuals involved.

Cover design: Cindy Kiple
Interior design: Beth Hagenberg
Images: Cover art by Susan Le Van represented by Moss Associates

ISBN 978-0-8308-4416-6 (print)
ISBN 978-0-8308-8404-9 (digital)

Printed in the United States of America ∞

Library of Congress Cataloging-in-Publication Data
Muehlhoff, Tim, 1961-
  I beg to differ : navigating difficult conversations with truth and love /
by Tim Muehlhoff.
      pages cm
  Includes bibliographical references.
  ISBN 978-0-8308-4416-6 (pbk. : alk. paper)
  1. Conflict management--Religious aspects—Christianity. 2.
Conversation—Religious aspects--Christianity. 3. Interpersonal
conflict—Religious aspects—Christianity. I. Title.
  BV4597.53.C58M84 2014
  241'.672—dc23
                                                                    2014004265

| P | 16 | 15 | 14 | 13 | 12 | 11 | 10 | 9 | 8 | 7 | 6 | 5 | | |
| Y | 27 | 26 | 25 | 24 | 23 | 22 | 21 | 20 | 19 | 18 | 17 | 16 | 15 |

Blessed are the peacemakers,
for they will be called children of God.

Contents

Foreword

The New Testament is relentless when it comes to unity. Jesus clearly calls his followers to communities released of contempt and anger—resolute in selfless devotion to the good of the other, even when the other is an enemy. And the model for the kind of unity he envisages for his disciples is none other than that found in the relationships between members of the Holy Trinity. The apostle Paul implores the church at Corinth to pursue a division-free and perfect unity of mind and judgment. The Ephesians are likewise called up into a life of loving, gentle and patient bearing of one with the other. The vision is clear. As followers of Jesus and his way, we're to find our way increasingly out of dissension and into loving unity with each other.

But how?

Here, as in other areas of deep human significance, God has elected to create for his children space for the joy of discovery. If we're to take seriously the injunction to pursue unity in our relationships, we must avail ourselves of the penetrating and life-giving wisdom that comes to us from the best reflections on human relatedness. We do well, then, to consider the study of communication as an accumulated body of wisdom and knowledge about how to progress toward the lofty biblical vision of unity.

As is always the case when availing oneself of an unfamiliar body of wisdom and knowledge, a guide is essential. Here is where this book comes in. Muehlhoff has given us an informed and accessible introduction to the art and science of communication in difficult situations. This book distills the theory of successful communication and offers the reader practical guidance for its application. The honest reader will frequently recognize herself in the difficult situations addressed in the book and will find in its pages practical suggestions for making progress.

Perhaps most importantly, one will find on these pages advice from an informed guide who practices what he preaches. I have found my way into disagreement with Tim on matters about which we both have passionate conviction. And I've seen the wisdom of this book transform those potentially divisive conversations into opportunities for mutual learning and growth.

My prayer is that you too will find your way into fruitful conversation in the context of disagreement and, in so doing, will find your way further up and further into the New Testament vision of unity.

Gregg Ten Elshof
Director, Center for Christian Thought, Biola University
Author, *I Told Me So: The Role of Self-Deception in Christian Living*

Acknowledgments

The thoughts found in this book have been evolving for many years, and there are many to thank. Tim Downs, thank you for listening to this communication strategy when it was in its earliest stage and I was a rookie trainer at the Communication Center. Your modeling of these concepts and encouragement to put it all on paper resulted in this publication. Jon Lunde, during our many long walks you patiently listened to incomplete ideas and scattered outlines. You greatly sharpened my thoughts. Deep appreciation goes to V. J. Vonk who read every word of this manuscript and gave timely proofreading and encouragement. Miss you. The love of communication theory that hopefully is evident in this book comes from my academic mentor and friend Julia Wood. Thank you for providing me with a solid foundation and the freedom to be me. The beauty of being at Biola University is having individuals such as Todd Lewis, Chris Grace, Rick Langer, Dorothy Calley, Melanie Whitcomb, Gregg Ten Elshof, Paul Spears, Craig Hazen and J. P. Moreland to give expert and timely advice. Special shout out goes to my COMM 474 students (Spring 2012) who willingly served as test subjects for this strategy for an entire semester. Your insights fill these pages. Al Hsu, I couldn't ask for a more accessible or insightful editor. Thank you for your patience. As always, deep appreciation goes to my wife and ministry partner who for the last twenty-three years has listened to my thoughts when they were raw, disjointed and unpublished. Noreen, without you none of this would be possible.

Introduction

Two stuffed manila folders sat in front of me.

It was difficult not to stare at them. I was meeting with a couple experiencing conflict. I had asked them to come prepared to identify and discuss troublesome topics, but nothing prepared me for what they brought. Vicki and Thomas arrived in separate cars and both walked into the restaurant carrying massive manila folders. Each of them had over the years separately compiled evidence to prove the other wrong. As each one described an issue, he or she would reach into a folder and produce supporting facts. The folders were stuffed with shopping receipts, phone records, photos, business vouchers, hastily scribbled notes and even transcripts of secretly recorded conversations.

I sat stunned. During our three-hour conversation I often thought of the proverb that states, "An offended brother is more unyielding than a fortified city" (Prov 18:19). Over the years this couple had grown discouraged in trying to resolve issues and now were only interested in fortifying entrenched positions.

Can you relate?

While few of us have gone so far as to fill folders with evidence against a person, we all can understand the frustration of having communication break down. All of us can think of conversations that ended badly. Heading in we hoped for the best but feared the worst—only to have the worst happen. Discussing this particular topic with this person sparked defensiveness, anger and raised voices. The result? A breach occurred and an argument broke out.

"Starting a quarrel," suggests an ancient writer, "is like breaching a dam" (Prov 17:14)—participants are swept away by powerful emotions. In the wake of the argument we are left with nagging questions: How can I remain faithful to my convictions but communicate in a way that produces dialogue, not uncivil debate? How can I balance truth and love when discussing difficult issues with people who disagree with me? And what if the person I'm struggling with is a spouse, family member, coworker or neighbor? The proverb admonishes me to drop the matter, not the relationship.

There is hope.

The same ancient writers who advise us to avoid quarrels also tell us that when our communication is pleasing to God, it's possible to live at peace even with our staunchest enemies (Prov 16:7). The realism of this verse is striking—people may not agree with us, but productive conversations marked by civility and peace are still possible. If civil communication can work with our enemies, then how much more with those we care about?

I Beg to Differ is more than a book about conflict; it is a book about communication between those who differ on significant points. Specifically, this book is for two types of individuals. First, it is for those who have attempted to discuss an issue with a friend, family member or coworker only to have the conversation deteriorate into a contentious exchange. The conversation may have left you shaken and gun-shy about bringing up the issue again. Better to live in silence or simmering anger than to revisit the topic and risk a similar result. Second, there are those who feel the need to discuss a topic with a person but envision the conversation going poorly. You desire to share Christ with a neighbor, discuss the budget with a spouse, or challenge a child's attitude, but before the first word is uttered you have psyched yourself out. How will you even begin to address the issue? Unsure, you avoid the topic.

I Beg to Differ introduces readers to a four-part communication strategy for the most difficult of conversations—those we wish to revisit and those we have yet to broach. The strategy centers on four essential questions that an individual must ask during an encounter with someone from a markedly different perspective. Gleaned from communication theory and the wisdom of the Scriptures, it values dialogue over debate, acknowledging and entering into a person's story, cultivating common ground, acknowledging doubts, and tailoring our communication to a particular person. These principles will not only work in face-to-face encounters but with the uncivil and often ugly exchanges that happen on Facebook or Twitter.

HOW WILL THIS BOOK HELP?

I Beg to Differ helps you prepare to enter difficult conversations by reclaiming the power of words (section one), learning to organize a conversation through an original four-part strategy (section two) and observing the application of this strategy to real life situations (section three). The following features make the book useful and easy to apply:

1. Each chapter introduces key principles found in communication theory such as cognitive complexity, the rule of reciprocation, constitutive rules, fundamental attribution error and agenda anxiety. Each of these ideas is presented in an accessible style.

2. *I Beg to Differ* is filled with illustrations not only from my own experience of speaking at marriage conferences, evangelism seminars, apologetic conferences and in the classroom, but illustrations from pop culture, leading communication experts and theologians.

3. At the close of each chapter, summary points help you remember key principles and questions from the chapter.

4. The core of the book (section two) centers on an original four-step communication strategy created during my graduate studies at

the University of North Carolina at Chapel Hill while I was seeking to understand and respond to diverse and sometimes disturbing views.

5. The final section includes three scenarios in which the principles of the book are applied to real life situations. How would a spouse talk about budget concerns without provoking the other? Can a Christian open a civil and productive dialogue with a follower of a different religious tradition? Without provoking her teenage son, how can a mother address concerns that he is too connected to social media and video games and not enough to the family? Each scenario takes the principles and theory of the book and shows readers how to apply them.

COMMUNICATING WITH INTEGRITY

Integrity, argues Bible expositor John Stott, is an indispensible part of learning to engage others. "Dialogue is a serious conversation in which we are prepared to listen and learn as well as to speak and teach. It is therefore an exercise in integrity."[1] Stott's observation prompts introspection. What type of communicator are we? As we engage in dialogue with others are we interested only in sharing our thoughts, or do we want to learn from others? Are we willing to listen as much as we speak? Do our convictions make us blind to areas of agreement with others? Can we honestly say we are open to compromise with those we care about, or is it only about winning an argument?

In the following pages I'll address those questions as we consider the delicate balance of listening, finding common ground with others, and responding in truth, love and integrity. We start with considering how our words influence others and ourselves.

SECTION ONE

Understanding Communication

In our desire to engage others we often rush past theory to focus on techniques. We're frustrated with another person and we just want to know what to say! Such impatience is understandable, but before we learn the how-to of communication we need to understand its ability to shape how we view ourselves and others, foster or elevate conflict, manage emotions and even draw us closer to God. Using communication effectively requires that we reclaim an appreciation for its complexity and power.

Reclaiming the Power of Words

Ellen Seidman is on a crusade. Her efforts have caught the attention of thousands of YouTube viewers, numerous educators, 250,000 petition signers and even President Obama. Her crusade doesn't focus on ending poverty, racism, global warming or sex trafficking. Her crusade is to end the use of a single word. Seidman and her followers seek to "spread the word to end the word." What's the word that has captured the attention of so many? "Retard."

Her efforts first started by posting a video on her blog, "Love That Max."[1] Max is Seidman's nine-year-old son who has cerebral palsy and has experienced the emotional pain and isolation caused by the "r" word. Watching Max withdraw from others and question his sense of worth due to this word has been heartbreaking and infuriating for this editor and mom. "It is a demeaning word even if it's meant as a joke," Seidman states, "because it spreads the idea that people who are cognitively impaired are either stupid or losers." Dr. Stephen B. Corbin, senior vice president for community impact of the Special Olympics, agrees. While Corbin acknowledges that "you can't ban terminology any more than you can ban thought," the goal is to educate others of the dehumanizing impact certain language has on others.[2]

The ancient writers whose words make up the book of Proverbs would agree with Corbin's assessment of the power of words, using vivid metaphors to describe the impact. "The words of the reckless pierce like swords" (Prov 12:18), they say, and a word spoken in the wrong way can "break a bone" (Prov 25:15). A person's spirit is easily crushed by a deceitful tongue (Prov 15:4). Just as the "north wind" can bring driving rain, so a "sly tongue" evokes an angry response (Prov 25:23). In plotting evil, a scoundrel's speech is like a "scorching fire" (Prov 16:27). Not only can negative words separate close friends (Prov 16:28), but a whole city can be disrupted by mockery (Prov 29:8). Old Testament scholar David Hubbard argues that what these ancient writers want us to most understand about language is that the tongue is "literally a lethal weapon—to others and ourselves."[3]

Yet in a technologically driven culture, the sheer volume of words being communicated can cause us to forget their power.[4] Facebook has more than a billion active users worldwide and is available in more than seventy languages. If Facebook were a country it would be the third largest in the world, lagging only behind China and India.[5] Today users on Twitter are sending more than two hundred million Tweets per day, or 2,315 per second.[6] YouTube reports that more than four billion videos are uploaded each month and that in 2011 it had more than one trillion views, or about 140 views for every person on earth.[7] Internet communication produces enough information to fill seven million DVDs every hour, with annual consumption predictions for 2015 at 966 exabytes.[8] To put this in perspective, a study by University of California Berkeley estimates that if all the words spoken by human beings were put into text form, they would take up merely five exabytes.[9]

A significant problem of modern society is its careless handling and tossing about of words. So how can we go about reclaiming respect for their power? In order to effectively negotiate a difficult conversation we must appreciate the ability of words to deeply confirm or disconfirm another person. Language is like a loaded gun, notes linguist Dwight Bolinger—it can be fired intentionally, but it can wound or kill just as surely when fired accidentally.[10]

The first step in crafting a difficult conversation is to reclaim a healthy respect for the power of words. When preparing to engage another individual in a challenging conversation, we must acknowledge and anticipate the impact our words could have. As Christian communicators, we must particularly embrace how seriously God takes human language.

GOD'S VIEW OF OUR SPEECH

In Proverbs 6 we encounter a remarkable list of what God finds detestable. The word translated "hate" in this passage is a Hebrew word often associated with disgust; it represents God's emotional reaction to certain human actions. These are the seven actions that evoke disgust from God: haughty eyes, a lying tongue, hands that shed innocent blood, a heart that devises wicked schemes, feet that are quick to shed evil, a false witness who pours out lies, and a person who stirs up dissension among brothers (Prov 6:17-19).[11]

It is interesting that of the seven traits mentioned, four have to do with our communication. "Haughty eyes" refers to an arrogant stance toward others, a nonverbal posture meant to intimidate and demean. A "lying tongue" and "false witness" both describe deceptive speech. And, finally, "a man who stirs up dissension among brothers" also refers to a form of communication detestable to God. Our first step toward respecting the power of communication is realizing the emotional response speech acts elicit from God. Far from being a stoic deity, God is deeply moved by our verbal and nonverbal choices.

Christ continues this emphasis on language when he declares that we all will be held accountable for every word uttered. At the end of our lives each of us will have to give an account of the millions of words we have spoken (Mt 12:36). Why are our words so important? Christ explains: "For the mouth speaks what the heart is full of" (Mt 12:34). For the biblical writers the heart represents the center of a person's personality, emotions, intellect and volition. It is through our communication with others that we glean a robust picture of them. While all communication exposes our inner person, Christ particularly isolates "careless" words that are spoken with little forethought (Mt 12:36 ESV).[12] The Greek word *argos*, translated "careless," refers to words we deem insignificant.

A few years ago my university started videotaping courses and posting lectures on iTunes U and YouTube. Two of my courses were selected, and the effect the process had on me was profound. Standing in front of my class and seeing the red light above the camera constantly reminded me that every word, joke, impromptu comment, critique and response to a student would be posted on the web the next day. Being recorded helped me understand that there are no careless comments—all are recorded and reflect who I am. When Christ tells us that our words reflect our heart, he was mirroring the attitude of many Roman and Greek philosophers who taught, *Talis oratio, quails vita* ("As the speech, so the life").[13]

A key motivation to reclaim the power of words is found in an unsettling statement about language found in the book of Proverbs: "The tongue has the power of life and death, and those who love it will eat its fruit" (Prov 18:21). Our speech has the power to build up or tear down others. In the next section we'll consider how our words can do this.

IMPARTING LIFE

Have you ever wondered why God created people? What do human communicators have to offer an all-knowing, all-wise and self-sufficient God? Perhaps, as many argue, we were primarily created to worship God. Yet the book of Isaiah informs us that the chief responsibility of six-winged angels called seraphs is to hover above God and shout out, "Holy, holy, holy" with such force that it shakes the doorposts of the temple (Isa 6:2-4). Surely we cannot out-worship seraphs. How can we engage God in a way that they can't? Václav Havel, former president of Czechoslavia and recipient of the United States President's Medal of Freedom, argues that one of God's greatest miracles is endowing us with the ability to communicate: "If the Word of God is the source of God's entire creation, then that part of God's creation which is the human race exists as such only thanks to another of God's miracles—the miracle of human speech."[14]

However, doesn't an all-knowing God already know our words before we speak them? David boldly states that "before a word is on my tongue you, LORD, know it completely" (Ps 139:4). So why even bother to communicate with God? The answer can be found in understanding that all communication exists on two levels—the content level and the relational level. The content level consists of the words we use to convey a message, while the relational level involves the amount of acknowledgment and respect between two individuals. When it comes to our content, God already comprehends our words as soon as we conceive of them and is intimately familiar with all of our thoughts (Ps 139:3). The uniqueness of human speech is that we can use words to interact with God on the relational level. The Scriptures inform us that "the LORD would speak to Moses face to face [acknowledgment], as one speaks to a friend [respect]" (Ex 33:11). And our ability to focus on the relational level is not limited to God. Life is imparted to others when we focus on the relational level with those we care about.

Understanding how words impart life plays a significant role in fostering community. Social critic Marilyn McEntyre argues that foundational to forming relationships with others is our ability to reclaim a sacred perspective of language.

A large almost sacramental sense of the import and efficacy of words can be found in early English usage, where conversation appears to have been a term that included and implied much more than it does now: to converse was to foster community, to commune with, to dwell in a place with others. Conversation was understood to be a life-sustaining practice, a blessing, and a craft to be cultivated for the common good.[15]

Imparting life through our words is a craft that involves the ability to offer a blessing rather than curse, seeking common ground rather than exploiting differences, and being committed to dwell with others in community. Seen in this way, our conversations can be life-sustaining.

One dramatic example of life-sustaining speech occurred during a churchwide prayer meeting I attended for a gravely ill pastor. While living in North Carolina, one of our pastors, Greg, was in the last stages of a long fight with cancer. In desperation, the church gathered to pray for healing. While Greg was too sick to attend, his two sons came to the meeting. For various reasons, the two boys had stopped attending church and were struggling with their faith. At the end of the meeting it was announced that Greg had unexpectedly shown up and wanted to address the crowd. He looked frail as he slowly walked to the microphone. In a weak voice he thanked us for coming and our prayers.

I will never forget what happened next. He specifically singled out two great men of faith who had stood by him during his illness and treatment, saying, "These godly men are here for me and I lean on their faith." We all assumed he was speaking about the other two pastors in the audience. He then invited the two men—his sons—to come up and join him. The father knew they were struggling with faith but made the decision to publically impart life into them by speaking to their reality as children of God. He reminded them who they were, not how they were currently struggling. Watching them stand next to their father—literally holding him up—I saw them transformed into Christlike comforters.

The same strategy is used by the apostle Paul in his shifts between the indicative and imperative moods in his writing. The indicative mood indicates the way things are, while the imperative mood focuses on the potential fulfilling of commands. For example, in his letter to the Colossian church the first two chapters are written in the indicative mood, reminding the readers of the freedoms they have in Christ. The next two chapters shift to the imperative mood, laying out commands for holy living.

The turning point in the letter comes when he starts chapter three by stating, "You have been raised with Christ [indicative]. . . . Put to death, therefore, whatever belongs to your earthly nature [imperative]" (Col 3:1, 5). Like Greg with his two sons, Paul reminds his readers of who they are and what they can become. Similarly, we impart life by reminding those with whom we struggle of unchanging truths—I am committed to you as a spouse, you are my daughter, we are both committed to this organization—as we seek to resolve differences and obey biblical commands to pursue peace.

Imparting life is not regulated to dramatic moments of battling cancer but can also be seen in simply offering a well-timed compliment. According to stereotype, women are inept at reading a map or parking a car. University of Warwick psychologist Zachary Estes set out to discover if a little confidence could overcome years of sexist jokes. He recruited 545 students for a series of experiments utilizing a 3-D rotation task that measured a person's ability to negotiate spatial challenges such as parallel parking. In one experiment, the researchers complimented or criticized a participant's skills in an unrelated task before administering the parking test.

When women were complimented before the parallel parking challenge, their confidence grew and their ability to park improved markedly. Estes concluded, "Our research suggests that by making a woman feel better about herself, she'll become better at spatial tasks. So a little bit of confidence-boosting may go a long way when it comes to reversing the car into a tight parking spot."[16] In other words, imparting life can have immediate and tangible results in influencing how others see themselves.

However, the proverb warns us that death is equally present in the tongue.

IMPARTING DEATH

In graphic language Paul warns his readers to stop imparting death: "If you bite and devour each other, watch out or you will be destroyed by each other" (Gal 5:15). Is it really possible to destroy another person emotionally or psychologically through words? Two powerful examples show the devastating impact our communication can have.

Kerry Fraser is one of hockey's most respected referees, and he describes how even the most hardened athlete can be deeply affected by words. Claude Lemieux made his living by scoring goals and taunting the opposition. He relished earning the title of most hated player in hockey. And it seemed that nothing bothered him. In 1995 he won the Conn Smyth Trophy as playoff MVP and led the New Jersey Devils in winning the Stanley Cup. He was also going through a bitter and public divorce. During one playoff game, an opposing player goaded Lemieux by referencing his divorce and estranged wife. During a stoppage of play, Lemieux skated up to Fraser, visibly shaken with tears in his eyes, pleading with him to tell this player to stop. Fraser notes that no physical injury could have stopped Lemieux in his quest for the cup. Yet verbal taunts not only took him off his game but emotionally unraveled him.

The same impact can be seen in racial slurs. In their book *Hate Hurts*, educators Caryl Stern-LaRossa and Ellen Hofmeimer-Bettmann collect narratives from students who have felt the devastating impact of racism. One teen shares his reaction to a slur: "One hint of black and they call you nigger. They say, 'All them look the same.' It hurts so much you just want to rip all your skin off and jump into a new one. You wish you were never that color and never born sometimes."[17] What's more, the ability to disseminate racial taunts and hurtful words has been augmented by technology. Cyberbullying is the use of information technology to intimidate, threaten or embarrass others, and one in ten parents worldwide reports that his or her child has been cyberbullied—twenty-four percent say they know of a child in their community who has been cyberbullied.[18] While there is no physical violence involved in these incidents, the words cause deep emotional scars with sometimes lethal effect. Researchers note that eight to twelve percent of middle school children who have been cyberbullied have contemplated taking their own lives after being exposed to such demeaning messages.[19]

Because words can hurt us deeply and even cause us to regret our existence, the apostle Paul firmly commands his readers to "not let any unwholesome talk come out of your mouths" (Eph 4:29). The word "unwholesome" suggests something rotten and unfit for use. During Paul's time this common word was used to describe food that had rotted and thus was quickly discarded. Paul is saying that communication infected with bitterness, anger, wrath, malice or slander should be viewed as rotted, unfit for use, and "put away" (Eph 4:31 ESV). To drive this point home to my students I once devised an odd assignment. During the first day of class I gave each student a ripe banana with instructions not to eat it. Rather, the students were to watch the banana rot during the semester. I also asked them to keep a journal recording observations about their speech. Here are some of their observations:

> "I have noticed a slow progression to rottenness that the banana is taking; I am sure that it will soon look absolutely horrendous, but for the moment it is not terrible. A blackening banana is only the beginning of the process of rotting. I do not like the thought of my mouth being on the same track as this banana."

"After much thought, I've come to realize that my tone can be just as rotted as my actual speech."

"One of the trickier things is humor because it often involves tearing people down but is covered in a joke. To me it is a deceptive way to tear people down and is just as bad."

"I noticed within myself that, as I become more desensitized to language, the more it allows me to become more lax in other areas. The more rotten a banana gets, the easier it is for it to ooze out all the rotten fruit."

As I watched my own banana begin to deteriorate, I was reminded to monitor my own words for the day. Midsemester my son found the plastic bag containing the banana and was so disgusted that he threw it away! His reaction mirrors Paul advice to us. To avoid infected speech, Paul tells us to get rid of it (Eph 4:31). In contrast, he tells us to edify each other by sharing only what is "helpful for building others up according to their needs, that it may benefit those who listen" (Eph 4:29). Edifying speech is both uplifting and instructive, affirming and corrective.

One student's reflection particularly stood out to me. In the following entry she considers how words shape her self-talk.

"I was reflecting on my speech today when I realized that this speech doesn't only pertain to what I say in a conversation or to others. Rotten speech also includes the things I tell myself. Though I do not say thoughts out loud, the things I think about myself can be rotten. Most of the things I tell myself are rotten."

How is it that words so deeply influence how we think about ourselves? Why are we so susceptible to their influence?

WHY DO WORDS HAVE SUCH AN IMPACT?

Cultural studies scholar Judith Butler asks these provocative questions: "Could language injure us if we were not, in some sense, linguistic beings who require language in order to be? Is our vulnerability to language a consequence of our being constituted within its terms?"[20] If Butler is correct that we are linguistic beings, how does language form us?

Communication scholars Ronald Adler, Lawrence Rosenfeld and Russell Proctor II argue that it is primarily through language that our self-concept and self-esteem are established. Self-concept is a collection of perceptions one holds about oneself. "One way to understand self-concept is to imagine a special mirror that not only reflects physical features, but also allows you to view other aspects of yourself—emotional states, talents, likes, dislikes, values, roles, and so on," these writers explain.[21] Self-esteem is a positive or negative evaluation of those personal perceptions. For example, while you may perceive yourself to be quiet in social settings (self-concept), do you view that as a positive or negative trait (self-esteem)? If you perceive yourself as an assertive communicator, do you view that as a good thing?

Most researchers agree that our self-concept does not exist at birth but arises as we communicate with those around us. The term "reflected appraisal" is used by researchers to suggest that we mirror the opinions of significant others, or those we deem important to us. Children growing up with stable, supportive parents tend to form healthy self-concepts, whereas children influenced by unstable, unsupportive parents tend to adopt negative self-concepts resulting in low self-esteem. Some researchers have even adopted the phrase "Michelangelo phenomenon" to express how our interaction with others emotionally sculpts our impression of who we are and how we view ourselves. Once our self-concept is firmly established, it is difficult to change. Individuals with low self-esteem often seek out and associate with others who have low self-esteem, and vice versa. When we encounter information that challenges our self-concept we often ignore or discount it.

But it is possible for our view of ourselves to change. There are four requirements, all rooted in communication, for this kind of change to occur. First, the person offering new information must be someone we deem competent; he or she must have the necessary ethos or credibility to change our self-concept. For example, while we appreciate our spouse's praise of our work, it might not carry the same weight as our supervisor's assessment. Second, the appraisal must be highly personal. It will mean little to our self-concept if our superior praises the entire department's work ethic rather than specifically highlighting our contribution. Third, appraisals must be reasonable in light of what we already think about ourselves. If a boss informs us that our report is the best-written and most insightful one he or she has read in thirty years, we may discount it as hyperbole. Simply put, we don't perceive that we are that good a writer. Last, appraisals must be both consistent and numerous. If our superior consistently tells us our reports are of high quality, we may begin to believe it and our self-concept is slowly altered.

If we are followers of Christ it can be meaningful to ask if God meets the four qualifications to impact self-concept. Do I view God as competent? Do I believe he loves me as a unique individual? In light of what I believe about myself (perhaps that I'm unlovable due to current struggles or lack of faith), do I think it reasonable that I am a beloved child of God? Do I consistently feel God's love toward me either via the Scriptures or the Holy Spirit?

A powerful step in reclaiming the power of words is embracing the idea that the self-concepts of those we care about and want to have meaningful conversations with can be significantly shaped by our words. A friend of mine who speaks at marriage conferences once said that eventually you get the spouse you deserve because you have molded him or her over time.

ANTICIPATING THE POWER OF WORDS

In the early 1920s a young communication scholar, I. A. Richards, wanted to help people understand why communication between two individuals often goes poorly. After years of research he argued that the foundational cause of interpersonal conflict was an inability to anticipate how one's words would affect a conversation. His remedy was a concept called "feedforward." Feedforward is the "process of anticipating the effects of communication and adapting to these anticipated effects in advance of actually communicating with others."[22]

In order to participate in this process we need to have an idea of a person's experiences, beliefs, values and core convictions before we engage him or her in conversation. How does this person feel about the topic I want to discuss? What is her conviction about the issue? How did she arrive at this conviction? How will she respond if I challenge it? In what areas do we agree? What words or tone will push her away? Simply put, feedforward is anticipatory feedback. If I don't know how my words will impact a person then I cannot adapt my communication effectively (we'll look at these questions more closely in section two). Rather than simply confronting the person, perhaps I need to gather information first.

One of the most dramatic examples of feedforward found in the Scriptures is James's admonishment to curb our tongues. He candidly tells us that our tongues are a "restless evil, full of deadly poison" (Jas 3:8). While he does not give us specific suggestions, he does ask us to engage in feedforward by vividly imagining the impact of our speech. He commands us to envision a forest that has been ravaged by one small spark—smell, taste and see the destruction. A few years ago our local high school was burned by California wildfires. The fires consumed one building, destroyed all shrubbery and landscaping, turned trees black, filled classrooms with thick, black smoke and covered the entire campus in ashes. Even today, when dropping off my kids, I can still see the blackened evidence of those fires. "The tongue also is a fire," James reminds us (Jas 3:6). In fact, it is a conduit of the very fires of hell. The key, he concludes, is to imagine or anticipate the verbal fire our words can cause and put a tight rein on the tongue.

CONCLUSION

Citizens of the town of Middleborough, Massachusetts, were so frustrated by public profanity that they voted 183 to 50 to issue tickets for public obscenity and profanity. The proponents of the law compared crude language to verbal vandalism and argued that words can rob others of a sense of peace and community.[23] What if you or I lived in a town that not only gave out tickets for negative or coarse communication but commendations for life-giving words? At the end of the year, would you or I have more citations or commendations? If we are serious about engaging those we care about in constructive conversations, we must first assess what type of communicator we've become—imparting life or death—and reclaim a respect for the damage our words can do to ourselves and others.

SUMMARY

The essential first step in handling difficult conversations is to reclaim a healthy respect for the power of words.

Power of words
Reckless words are like a piercing sword (Prov 12:18) that can crush a person's spirit (Prov 15:4) or even break a bone (Prov 25:15).

The tongue is a lethal weapon to others and ourselves.

God's view of our speech
Four communicative acts disgust God: haughty eyes, a lying tongue, a false witness and a person who stirs up dissension (Prov 6:17-19).

At the end of our lives we will held accountable for every careless word uttered (Mt 12:36).

Words impart life
The uniqueness of human speech is that we can use words to impart life to both God and others.

In early English usage to converse with a person was a life-sustaining practice.

Words impart death

The apostle Paul commands us not to let any unwholesome talk come out of our mouths (Eph 4:29).

Unwholesome speech equals rotted communication filled with anger, bitterness, malice and slander.

Why do words have such impact?

"Reflected appraisal" means we tend to mirror the opinions of significant others.

The "Michelangelo phenomenon" is the idea that interaction with others sculpts our impression of who we think we are and how we think others view us.

There are four requirements for a person's appraisal to change how we view ourselves: (1) the person is someone we deem important, (2) the appraisal is highly personal, (3) the appraisal is reasonable, and (4) the appraisal is consistent and numerous.

Anticipating the power of words

"Feedforward" means anticipating the effects of our communication on others and adapting our speech in advance.

What Causes Verbal Dams to Rupture?

"Are you sure you want to do that?"

Slowly I'd take my hand off the chess piece I was about to move. During the year of ministry I spent in Lithuania with a small team of American believers, we were constantly looking for ways to fight off boredom caused by the frigid weather outside and the sporadic Russian television reception inside our small apartment. To pass time I'd taken up playing chess with my friend Mark. While Mark was an experienced player, I was new to the complexities of chess. Just as I was about to make a move, Mark would clear his throat in warning. "Be careful," he said. "What you are about to do will cause problems later. In chess, there are no small moves." Most times he was spot on. Seemingly innocuous moves would get me in trouble later.

I found the same to be true in my role as team leader for our group of six Americans. While trying to adjust to life abroad, mesh differing ministry philosophies, and adapt to conflicting personalities, I discovered that seemingly innocuous individual moves deeply affected the entire team. To work together effectively we had to learn to consider the ramifications of our actions. Asking, "Am I sure I want to do that?" applied equally to chess and relationships.

In this chapter we'll consider how our actions can alleviate or foster conflict. Specifically, we'll consider the reality of conflict and some of the most common precursors to disagreement, bitterness and relational rupture. If we are to be successful in cultivating healthy conversations, we need to understand the variables that cause conversation to break down.

THE REALITY OF CONFLICT

Research shows that conflict is present even in the best of relationships. In one study, college students were asked to keep a record of their interactions with others and report any arguments. The average student experienced seven arguments a week. Some exchanges were one-time disagreements, while others were recurring disputes that played out over weeks, months and even years.[1] Other research shows that disagreement among friends occurs on average once or twice a day.[2] Family interaction, particularly at the dinner table, is particularly fertile ground for tension and conflict. Family scholar Sam Vuchinich recorded the dinnertime conversations of fifty-two families and identified an average of 3.3 disagreements or arguments during each meal.[3] While these disagreements are not often shouting matches, they are still times of contention. Perhaps your family doubles or even triples the average.

This research shows that interpersonal conflict is, at some level, inevitable. Therefore we should not be surprised when conflict occurs in our relationships, even with fellow Christians. Relational conflict is a common theme in the Scriptures. While the apostle Paul exhorts the Philippians to "make my joy complete by being like-minded" and be "one in spirit and of one mind" (Phil 2:2), he still has to intervene in a disagreement between Euodia and Syntyche and ask them to "be of the same mind in the Lord" (Phil 4:2). Paul tells believers at Corinth that they have been called to be holy "together with all those everywhere who call on the name of our Lord Jesus Christ" (1 Cor 1:2). Yet nine verses later he writes that he has learned there are "quarrels among you" (1 Cor 1:11). Paul himself experienced conflict with Peter over Peter's decision to separate from Gentile Christians and eat only with Jewish Christians (Gal 2:11-14). Just as there are no perfect people outside the church, there are none inside.

Because disagreement is inevitable, we need to understand the factors that fuel it. While the following list is not exhaustive, it contains common antecedents that lay the groundwork for interpersonal conflict.

A POOR COMMUNICATION CLIMATE

Imagine taking a run when the heat index is over a hundred degrees or going ahead with plans for a family picnic in the middle of a thunderstorm. There's a reason advertisements for fireworks displays always include the disclaimer "weather permitting." Mother Nature will not be ignored and we are wise to adjust our behavior to hers. The same is true with communication. As soon as two people start to talk, a communication climate is formed that is just as real as the weather outside your door—and just as impossible to ignore. A key step to improving communication and reducing conflict is to understand the overall climate of the relationship in which the communication takes place.[4]

A communication climate is the overarching sense of value and satisfaction individuals feel as they interact with each other and go about daily activities. In other words, it's not "what we communicate about that shapes a relational climate," communication experts note, "as much as how we speak and act toward one another."[5] Communication climates consist of four crucial elements: acknowledgement, expectations, trust and commitment. Each plays a role in the health of a climate and, if ignored, can contribute to conflict.

Acknowledgment. Acknowledging another person is perhaps the most confirming form of communication and the most rare. We acknowledge another person when we take time to seek out and attend to his or her perspective. Acknowledgment is often expressed by eye contact, touching, asking questions and allowing a person to speak uninterrupted. Philosopher William James once speculated that the worst punishment he could think of was to exist in a community yet remain unnoticed by others. Acknowledging another person's perspective does not mean we necessarily condone or agree with it. Rather, we simply recognize the validity and uniqueness of that perspective. To notice and engage another person as a unique and irreplaceable individual is a deeply encouraging form of interaction. Conversely, if we regularly feel that our perspective is not being acknowledged in a relationship, the climate will quickly deteriorate.

Trust. If the communication climate is marked by mistrust, a person "begins to question what is stated and looks for an unstated real answer, which begins a cycle of distrust and suspicion," communication researchers note.[6] And this lack of trust will compromise any attempt to communicate or resolve differences effectively. For this reason the apostle Paul tells the believers at Ephesus that they should "put off falsehood and speak truthfully" to others (Eph 4:25). The book of Proverbs often contrasts honesty with lying. Referring to a Persian custom of greeting trusted friends with a kiss, the writer states that an "honest answer is like a kiss on the lips" (Prov 24:26). A lying tongue, on the other hand, not only destroys trust but imparts pain and hate to the recipient (Prov 26:28). Researchers continually identify trust as a foundational characteristic of healthy communication climates.[7]

Expectations. Relationships are filled with expectations. Words like "husband," "wife," "son," "daughter," "grandparent," "relative," "manager," "subordinate," "coworker," "pastor," and "brother" or "sister in Christ" are all highly personalized concepts shaped by spoken and unspoken expectations. While I may not explicitly express to my office manager that he or she should be interested in my family, I will be disappointed if the only things we ever discuss are business-related topics. If my child is hospitalized, do I expect the senior pastor to make a visit or am I content to see the associate pastor? When my daughter goes off to college, do I expect daily, weekly or monthly correspondence? Do I expect to hear from her only when she needs money? If I attempt to bring up spiritual issues with a coworker, do I expect him to be offended or grateful? Expectations have a powerful way of setting a positive or negative tone in a relationship.

Commitment. "The hallmark of commitment," notes relationship expert Julia Wood, is "the assumption of a future."[8] Our climates will suffer if we carry a nagging doubt that if the relationship gets difficult or the conflict too intense, the relationship may end. Individuals who lack confidence in this area often employ the exit response to conflict, wherein conflict is avoided at all costs for fear of crippling or ending the relationship. Conversely, psychologists have long noted how commitment between individuals fosters feelings of empowerment and positive self-image.

DIFFERING VIEWS OF REALITY

Communication scholars believe that some—maybe even most—of reality is created by our perception. While this statement may sound surprising, it becomes less so when we realize that there are two levels of reality. First-order realities are observable aspects of people, things and situations. Second-order realities are the meanings we attach to people, things and situations.[9] Seldom do first-order realities cause conflict. However, second-order realities often do. Consider how Barack Obama stirred up controversy by not wearing a lapel pin of the American flag (first-order reality) while campaigning for his presidential run. His political opponents quickly seized on that omission and argued that the absence of the pin signified a lack of patriotism (second-order reality). The absence of the pin was undeniable, but what it meant became a national debate.

My favorite example of second-order realities is a picture of a burly, bare-chested man standing by the Grand Canyon wearing nothing but a smile and a pink tutu. When I show my students the picture, I ask them to offer first-order observations. "What's to say?" comments one student. "The dude is wearing a pink ballet skirt. He's weird." While the tutu is undeniable, what is his reason for wearing it? What second-order meaning does it have for him?

In 2006, Bob Carey's wife was diagnosed with breast cancer. It was particularly devastating news since Linda had already beaten cancer in 2003. The thought of going through chemotherapy again was overwhelming for both of them. In an effort to cheer Linda up, Bob decided to do something thoughtful and slightly embarrassing. He decided that while traveling on business trips he would wear a pink tutu to scenic destinations and have someone take his picture so he could text it to Linda while she was isolated receiving treatment. The color pink represents solidarity with cancer survivors, while the tutu was chosen for its sheer absurdity. When Linda saw the pictures she couldn't stop laughing. Since then Bob has written a book, *Ballerina*, that chronicles his trek across the country sporting the tutu in unlikely places. Through the Tutu Project he continues to raise awareness and money in the fight against cancer. Understanding Bob's second-order meaning for the tutu completely transformed how my class viewed him and his seemingly odd actions.

Second-order realities are not limited to politics or cancer awareness. They have a profound impact in how we interpret and respond to each other's actions. While I was speaking at a marriage conference a couple came up to me and voiced their displeasure with each other. "He never acknowledges the small things I do to encourage him," she said with arms folded. "Every morning when I brush my teeth I make sure to put toothpaste on his brush. It's my way of letting him know I'm thinking of him." The husband's sarcastic laugh took me by surprise.

"You disagree," I said.

"It's her subtle way of bossing me around," he replied. "As if I need to be reminded to brush my own teeth. I'm not a child!"

Toothpaste on a brush was a simple first-order reality, but what it meant was driving this couple apart. Communication scholars Adler, Rosenfeld and Proctor conclude that communication problems arise "when we don't share second-order realities, especially when we don't realize that these views of the world are personal constructions, not objective facts."[10] Effective communication is a matter of understanding that what a person does—coming home late, not returning a text, leaving dishes in the sink—are merely what philosopher John Searle calls "brute facts" that require us to assign meaning to them. A coworker is a late to a meeting you are leading. His lateness is merely a raw fact that has to be interpreted. Was he purposefully disrespectful or merely running late? Searle's point is that meanings—our interpretations—are not inherently attached to actions. ✒

One of the most important forms of first-order realities is nonverbal communication. In a study that sent shock waves among communication experts, psychologist Albert Mehrabian claimed that ninety-three percent of the emotional force of a message came through nonverbal channels, leaving only seven percent to our words.[11] His claim starts to gain credence when you realize that nonverbal communication includes eyes, face, posture, gestures, touch, use of personal space, tone of voice, physical features, style of dress, personal artifacts and even silence. Such powerful factors lead communication scholars to assert that a person, regardless of his or her intentions, cannot *not* communicate. While it is possible to stop verbal communication, nonverbal communication is continuous and nearly impossible to control. The mere fact that I've stopped talking is a form of nonverbal communication that is open to interpretation. Is my silence evidence of boredom, tiredness or anger?

To make matters even more complex, most of us are unaware of the subtleties of our own nonverbal communication.[12] When I train people in public speaking I often videotape them. Clients are shocked to see how they come across to the audience. They are not alone. Studies show that most of us are not conscious of how or what we communicate nonverbally. The difficulty is compounded when those with whom we converse assign meaning to the non-verbal acts we're not even conscious of doing.

C. S. Lewis's classic *The Screwtape Letters* is an attempt to creatively expose demonic strategy in which a senior devil advises his underling on how to conjure conflict among humans. This entry focuses on the power nonverbal actions play in driving a wedge between a son and his mother:

> When two humans have lived together for many years, it usually happens that each has tones of voice and expressions of face which are almost unendurably irritating to the other. . . . Let him assume that she knows how annoying it is and does it to annoy—if you know your job he will not notice the immense improbability of the assumption.[13]

The son makes the mistake of believing that his mother's tone of voice or facial expression is consciously done to annoy him. We often make the same mistake when we believe that our interpretation of a brute fact is unequivocally correct.

To promote productive conversations, we need to examine the meanings we give to the actions of others through a process called perception-checking. This crucial process has three distinct steps. First, we provide a description of the behavior in question. Second, we offer two possible interpretations of the behavior. Third, we ask for clarification about how to interpret the behavior.

For example, say your family finally finds a night when everyone is home. You decide to make dinner so the family can reconnect. During dinner your teenage daughter keeps checking text messages (first-order reality), which frustrates you immensely because you're sure it's a sign that she'd rather be somewhere else (second-order reality). The mistake would be to leave your interpretation unchecked and allow your anger toward her to grow. Instead, you could try saying, "Kate, you keep checking your phone. Is everything OK with your friends, or are you kind of bored?"

She may tell you that one of her friends is having a hard time or has just received some exciting news she has to share. If that's the case, it may be worth it to allow Kate to wrap up the conversation with one or two more texts so she can focus on dinner. If she tells you she's bored, thank her for her honesty and attempt to apply the steps we'll discuss later in the book.

LACK OF CREDIBILITY

The Greek philosopher Aristotle was fascinated with communication. His book *On Rhetoric* focuses particularly on how we can effectively persuade other people through speech. He concludes that the single greatest factor is a speaker's ethos, or credibility. The word "credibility" comes from the Latin *credere*, which means "to believe." When I'm listening to the opinions of another person, do I tend to believe what he or she is saying?

Aristotle breaks ethos down into three components. The first is intelligence. Do I believe you know the facts of the situation or are you mistaken on key issues? Consider the emergence of fact-checkers in modern politics. As soon as a politician makes a claim in a speech or debate, fact-checkers quickly seek to validate or disprove it. Two MIT graduates have even created a truth application for your phone that will allow you to fact-check political advertisements. Much like the Shazam app identifies music when you place your cell phone near a song being played, this app will allow you to identify and check political ads. The truth app listens to a political advertisement and informs the user who paid for the ad and how much it costs, and it checks nonpartisan databases to verify the ad's claims.

Likewise, we each have our own personal truth app when we listen to others. As a person is speaking, we constantly check his or her facts against databases we've accumulated over time. These databases are the product of our own personal experiences, experts we trust, sources we think are credible, and our own selective and often faulty memories. Disagreement arises when the perspective being offered does not match up to our version of the facts.

A friend of mine was being interviewed on local television about the rise of atheism. He argued that atheism originated in the city because every farmer intuitively knows that rain, sunshine and crops comes from God. The interviewer responded, "You can't possibly know that!" Do you see what happened? As soon as my friend made his assertion, the host sifted through her nonreligious truth app and found his view unbelievable. As human fact-checkers we must be careful to understand and identify the biases inherent in our judgment of facts.

The second component of ethos is virtue. While the person speaking may know the facts of a particular situation, he may live a life that undermines his credibility. Paul informs Christians in Corinth that they are ambassadors for Christ and have received the ministry of reconciliation. As ambassadors they need to know the facts of who Christ is and how to reconcile others to him. He concludes by exhorting them to live a life worthy of Christ so "our ministry will not be discredited" (2 Cor 6:3). These believers were a reflection of Paul's virtue in the Aristotelian sense.

In the same way, we will discount the convictions of another person if we perceive he or she does not live up to her own standards. I once had a coworker who was a phenomenal employee but who regularly struggled with lateness. After I was late to an important meeting he confronted me. While he had every right to call me out on my tardiness, it was hard to receive his rebuke because of his own tendency to be late. To me, he had lost his credibility to speak on this issue.

The last component of ethos is goodwill. While a speaker may have his or her facts straight and live a life of virtue, how the message is presented can destroy credibility. If we judge the mode of communication as being harsh or abusive, we will ignore the message. As we discussed in the last chapter, all communication exists on both a content level and a relational level. The relational level focuses on the amount of respect and acknowledgment between individuals. If I perceive that you are addressing me in a disrespectful way, conflict will deepen. "A harsh word stirs up anger," argue the ancient writers of the book of Proverbs (Prov 15:1). It is a perspective Paul affirms when he informs readers that truth must always be accompanied by love (Eph 4:15).

RELATIONAL TRANSGRESSIONS

When my oldest son moved into his dormitory at the start of his freshman year, the first thing he and his new roommate did was set boundaries. This is my desk, my bed, my closet and my general personal space. Problems arise when one roommate transgresses, or oversteps his bounds.

The word "transgression" comes from a late Middle English word that means "stepping across." And this stepping across of boundaries occurs in all relationships when implicit or explicit rules are broken. These relational rules, scholars say, are the "musts, oughts, and shoulds that guide an individual's behavioral choices and that shape the interpretations of and attributions assigned to the behaviors of others."[14] These rules fall into four general categories:

Secrecy-privacy. The use or misuse of personal information can be a powerful form of transgression. What I tell you in confidence must stay between us. Can I trust you to be my confidant or do I need to be guarded in what I share? On the other hand, do I believe that you are withholding information from me?

Commitment. Simply put, will you make good on your promises? If you tell me something is going to get done, will it? How easy is it for you to break a promise? Is your word your bond? Notice how strongly this category and the one above relate to the trust and commitment components of a communication climate. If transgressions happen regularly in these areas, the climate will quickly become unhealthy and conflict will escalate.

Privileging the relationship. We assume in our most important relationships that each person will give priority to the relationship. Do you use your disposable time with me or another person? Am I investing more emotional energy in this relationship than you are? Has our relationship become one-sided? *Interaction management.* When we argue, do we do it fairly? Do either of us engage in emotional, physical or verbal abuse? Are we respectful of each other's opinions even when we disagree?

While transgressions can happen in each of these categories, scholars identify one transgression that is particularly damaging to a relationship—sexual infidelity made public. Few of us will forget the look of pain and betrayal etched in the faces of Sandra Bullock, Demi Moore and Elin Nordegren when the affairs of their husbands—Jesse James, Ashton Kutcher and Tiger Woods—became public. The public embarrassment that occurs when details emerge will cripple a relationship. Individuals who desire to pursue reconciliation after a relational transgression will need to craft discussions carefully in order to foster understanding, healing and forgiveness.

LACK OF PHATIC COMMUNICATION

When we're engaged in disagreements over topics that are important to us, it's easy to be consumed by the issues at stake. These conversations, in which we attempt to persuade the other person of our point of view, are called "emphatic communication." This type of communication is often dramatic, passionate, intense and memorable and has been the target of much research. However, it is not the only form of communication. After spending years studying how people of diverse cultures interact, anthropologist Bronislaw Malinowski discovered a subtle form of communication that is indispensible to healthy relationships. In 1923 he came up with the phrase "phatic communication" to refer to small talk that builds relationships.[15]

The term caught on and has been the focus of intense study among scholars, who define phatic communication as "the seemingly routine, undramatic, unremarkable communication that fills people's days and relationships."[16] Simply put, phatic communication is the small talk that makes significant communication possible.

While I was in college I became good friends with a fellow communication major who was an outspoken atheist. We spent hours debating the existence of God, the reliability of the Bible, Jesus' divinity, how a good God can allow evil, and what really happens when we die. These conversations would last into the early morning hours and often became heated. How could such a friendship last with such emphatic disagreement? It lasted because that's not all we talked about. Our debates were offset with epic Ping-Pong games, midnight runs to the local sub shop, talk of girls, dissing each other's favorite sport teams (I was born in Michigan and he in Ohio—enough said), and just goofing off. As we would pass each other in the dorm, we'd ask if there had been a change in the other's belief about God.

"Nope!" was the response.

"Just checking," we'd say, continuing to walk.

Those seemingly insignificant exchanges served as a much-needed break from our debates about God. If every conversation we have with others is about the issues that divide us, the intensity will hurt the communication climate. "Phatic speech is indispensible," argues social critic Umberto Eco, "precisely because it keeps the possibility of communication in working order, for the purpose of other and more substantial communications."[17] If all you and your spouse, child or coworker do is debate and argue, then perhaps a wise thing to do would be to insert regular moments of phatic talk. Phatic communication allows communicators to step back from the issues, take an emotional break, and keep the lines of communication open.

LATENT CONFLICT

When a friend of mine talks about disagreement with her teenage daughter, she often says, "It's not about the muffins." Here's why.

One morning before school my friend's daughter shouted at her, "I hate muffins!" and bolted out the door. With the sound of the slamming door still ringing in her ears, my friend looked at the muffins she'd baked for breakfast. The night before she had informed her daughter of a curfew that was going into effect that coming weekend. "That outburst was about many things," she said to me, "but I'm pretty sure it's not about muffins." What my friend was experiencing is something communication scholars call "latent conflict."

Most conflict begins with a latency period in which tension or disagreement exists between individuals but is not expressed. Tension, anger or hurt may exist consciously or subconsciously and last for long periods before coming out. In fact, it may never emerge explicitly. Two significant problems are associated with latent conflict. First, individuals may adopt the "neglect response," which denies or minimizes problems, disagreements, anger, tension and other problems. For whatever reason, people who are angry with each other may decide not to discuss the tension, allowing the anger or disagreement to build up. For example, when Katie Couric asked supermodel Heidi Klum to pinpoint the primary reason she couldn't salvage her marriage with pop singer Seal, Klum explained that her approach was not to address conflict but to smile, push it away and move on.[18] Eventually the approach backfired and the marriage fell apart.

Second, latent conflict often results in the practice of "kitchen-sinking." Once a conflict begins, everything that has been stored up gets thrown in. Theorists often call this the "one-sentence explosion." For example, if my friend's daughter finally expresses her displeasure at the new weekend curfew, she may also explode with the anger she feels toward other family rules..The problem is that multiple issues now compound one issue—displeasure at a curfew.

In an attempt to curb latent conflict, the apostle Paul commands readers to "not let the sun go down while you are still angry" (Eph 4:26). Paul is paraphrasing a similar idea expressed in the Psalms:

"In your anger do not sin; when you are on your beds, search your hearts and be silent" (Ps 4:4 NIV footnote). Notice that the focus in both passages is on dealing with anger, not resolving conflict.

Many have misinterpreted Paul to mean that the conflict we are facing needs to be dealt with fully before we go to sleep. In most situations resolving conflict quickly is not only impractical but can worsen it. Rather Paul is admonishing us to deal with our latent or overt anger promptly so as to not let it take root. This may involve a number of actions: asking God to show us the cause of anger, confessing unloving thoughts or actions, starting a spiritual discipline to address our feelings, getting godly advice, or reaching out to the person who caused such powerful feelings. Notice that the primary motivation Paul gives for dealing with anger is to avoid giving the devil "a foothold" (Eph 4:27).

CONCLUSION

Each of the antecedents of conflict discussed above was present in my discussion with the couple armed with manila folders. As Vicki and Thomas were still rummaging through their folders for conclusive evidence against each other, I informed them that I had to leave. Thomas followed me to my car in an attempt to convince me with one last document. As my frustration grew and his voice started to rise, I climbed into my car. Through a cracked window he told me it's hard to control his anger when discussing his marriage. Most of us can relate. If we are honest, controlling surging emotions is one of the greatest obstacles to cultivating healthy discussion and is the topic of our next chapter.

SUMMARY

Conflict is present in all relationships. Keep in mind the following causes:

Poor communication climate
Conflict is compounded when there are lack of acknowledgment, unmet expectations, broken trust and fluctuating commitment levels in a relationship.

Differing views of reality
First-order realities are observable aspects of people, things or situations. Second-order realities are the meanings we attach to people, things and situations. There are no raw facts, only the meaning we attach to them.

Lack of credibility
Intelligence: do I believe you know the facts of the situation?

Virtue: do you live a life that disqualifies you from making judgment?

Goodwill: is your communication harsh, mean or abusive?

Relational transgressions
Secrecy-privacy: personal information has been misused.

Commitment: does a person make good on promises?

Privileging the relationship: does this person give priority to the relationship?

Interaction management: when we argue, do we do it fairly?

Lack of phatic communication
Small talk is eliminated and every conversation starts and stops with an attempt to persuade the other of his or her point of view.

Latent conflict
Tension, anger or hurt may exist consciously or subconsciously and last for long periods of time before coming out.

Kitchen-sinking: once conflict begins, everything that has been stored up is thrown in.

Managing and Expressing Emotions in the Midst of Disagreement

As President Obama passionately described his health plan to the House of Representatives, he was abruptly and unceremoniously interrupted.

"You lie!" shouted Republican Representative Joe Wilson.

A murmur swept through the House and all eyes focused on Wilson. After the speech the reaction to his outburst was terse. "I've never seen anything like it!" said North Dakota Representative Earl Pomeroy. John McCain called it "utterly disrespectful." While presidents are often criticized, few have been so harshly addressed in public.

"We do not invite the president of the United States to the House of Representatives and hurl insults," Pomeroy concluded. Later Wilson apologized, explaining that his comment was inappropriate and that he let his emotions get the best of him.

One of the difficulties we encounter when discussing topics we're passionate about is that our emotions often derail or inflame the conversation. (Imagine Representative Wilson trying to discuss healthcare with the president after his outburst.) Emotions must be dealt with effectively, states Roger Fisher, founder of the Harvard Negotiation Project and lead advisor for the negotiations between the United States and Iran concerning the release of fifty-two American hostages in 1979. From that experience and other difficult negotiations he writes:

> None of us is spared the reality of emotions. They can ruin any possibility of a wise agreement. They can turn an amicable relationship into a long-lasting feud where everybody gets hurt. And they can sour hopes for a fair settlement.[1]

The difference between an amicable resolution and a long-lasting feud is, in part, our ability to manage our emotions in the heat of the moment. Due to the power of our emotions to influence conversations, it is wise to consider the role they play in communication, understand how they are shaped, and examine strategies for effectively using our emotions in our interactions. Before we consider how they influence our communication, we'll address a common misconception concerning emotions.

MISCONCEPTIONS

Many of us believe that the worst thing we can do during a disagreement is to become emotional. Emotions are unpredictable, we think, and they'll undermine our ability to discuss an issue objectively and dispassionately; therefore we need to suppress our emotions or ignore them while seeking to resolve a disagreement.

This view has many flaws. First, it's simply not possible. "You cannot stop having emotions any more than you can stop having thoughts," Fisher writes.[2] The goal of a balanced communicator is to properly manage and express both thoughts and emotions. When the apostle Paul encourages Christians at Ephesus to pursue Christ, he doesn't pray merely that their intellect or rationale would be enlightened by God. Rather, he prays that the "eyes of your heart may be enlightened" (Eph 1:18). In Hebrew the word "heart" means all of an individual—intellect, emotions, body and will. God wants all of our selves to be engaged in our pursuit of him.

The same is true when we approach conflict. To deny or push aside our emotions is to enter into a conversation only partially. In his early study of communication climates, Jack Gibb argued that approaching another person with detached neutrality—ignoring or failing to acknowledge that person's emotions—was sure to turn a communication climate negative.[3] The surest way to inflame another person's emotion is to belittle or ignore it. As we will see in section two, expressing and acknowledging emotions correctly is foundational to healthy conversation.

Second, the problem with suppressing our emotions during a charged conversation is that in the process we may also suppress our motivation to resolve the conflict. In his massive five-hundred-page treatise *On Religious Affections*, the great Puritan preacher Jonathan Edwards writes that the nature of human beings is to be inactive unless somehow motivated by a powerful feeling or affection. Feelings of hatred, love, passion, hopefulness, hopelessness and anger serve as a spring of action that propel us forward to duty and others. If we mistakenly suppress our emotions, we may also short-circuit the very mechanism that launches us toward resolution. Often within difficult conversations our emotions—desire to reconcile, address an injustice, resolve conflict, share Christ's love—provide the spring of action that keeps us in the conversation.

Third, emotions are a powerful indicator that individuals still care about each other and the relationship. I often tell my students that the opposite of love is not hate but indifference. I don't hate individuals I'm indifferent to or who do not matter to me. Why waste the emotional effort? My anger is more likely to arise in response to people who mean something to me—a boss, spouse, coworker, child or other close individual. Marriage researcher John Gottman says he can help a couple if one thing is present within that troubled relationship: emotion. If individuals are still expressing feelings—even inappropriately—the marriage can be helped because emotions are indicators of concern for each other. "Stonewalling" is the term Gottman uses to describe a relationship in which neither person has emotion or feeling for the other. He concludes that if stonewalling continues and emotions do not return, that relationship is destined for divorce. Tragically, his predictions are true ninety-one percent of the time.[4]

Last, the reason we don't suppress or deny our emotions is that God didn't suppress his while engaging with us. In the Scriptures we encounter a God who is unchanging, powerful, holy and emotional.

GOD AND EMOTIONS

How do you respond to the idea that, in addition to being holy and powerful, God is emotional? We tend to read that word in a negative sense as a sign of not being in control. Does God have emotions and do they move him? Many early Christian leaders and theologians answered in the negative. Their answer was an attempt to separate the Christian God from the scandalous behavior of Greek gods such as Zeus, who handed out vengeance in fits of rage. Assigning emotions to God seemed to these early leaders to weaken God and make him too human. Thus the Council of Chalcedon (A.D. 451) concluded that God could not suffer or be emotionally moved by events or persons. If God isn't moved by emotions, then neither should we be. The difficulty with such a position is that it doesn't mesh with the picture of God and Jesus we find in the Scriptures.

After seeing a Christian friend experience deep personal suffering and the doubt that ensued, author Philip Yancey sought to understand how God responds to our pain. To find the answer he spent two weeks in an isolated cabin in Colorado reading the Scriptures cover to cover. His question: Is God stoic in the presence of our pain? When the two weeks were over Yancey offered this assessment:

Simply reading the Bible, I encountered not a misty vapor but an actual Person. A Person as unique and distinctive and colorful as any person I know. God has deep emotions; he feels delight and frustration and anger. In the Prophets he weeps and moans with pain, even comparing himself to a woman giving birth: "I cry out, I gasp and pant." . . . I know, I know, the word "anthropomorphism" is supposed to explain all those humanlike characteristics. But surely the images God "borrows" from human experience point to an even stronger reality.[5]

The emotions of God are on full display when we consider Jesus, who is the "image of the invisible God" (Col 1:15). The portrait of Jesus in the New Testament is that of a Savior who exhibits a keen intellect and vibrant emotions such as surprise, joy, sorrow, grief, amazement, indignation and so on. Consider the depictions of Jesus found in the Gospel of Mark. In one scene, the Pharisees challenge Jesus regarding his intention to heal on the Sabbath. In response, Jesus is angry and deeply distressed at their callous reaction to the man with a deformed hand who is seeking help (Mk 3:5).

Later, as Jesus faces his impending death while in Gethsemane, raw emotion pours out of him as he collapses to the ground and declares, "My soul is overwhelmed with sorrow to the point of death" (Mk 14:34). This admission was so uncharacteristic of one claiming to be the Messiah that early Christian apologists used it as evidence that stories of Christ had not been altered. If followers of Jesus were editing stories to make Christ more credible, then surely his emotional outburst would have been deleted as a sign of weakness.

And also, when Jesus encounters a temple system that turns worship into a moneymaking enterprise and unnecessarily burdens the poor, Jesus becomes angry and takes action. He overturns tables and benches, declaring that he will not tolerate a house of prayer being turned into a "den of robbers" (Mk 11:17). Ancient philosophers identified anger as "the moral emotion" because it is often based on a reflective judgment that we have been wronged or an injustice has occurred. That day in the temple Jesus judged individuals being wronged by a corrupt system, and he acted quickly.

In our desire to be effective communicators we must embrace and express our emotions in ways that mirror and honor Christ. New Testament scholar Walter Hansen observes:

> In our quest to be like Jesus we often overlook his emotions. Jesus reveals what it means to be fully human and made in the image of God. His emotions reflect the image of God without any deficiency or distortion. When we compare our own emotional lives to his, we become aware of our need for a transformation of our emotions so that we can be fully human, as he is.[6]

In order for our emotions to be transformed, we need to first understand the many factors that shape them.

PERCEPTION AND EMOTIONS

While doing relief work in Nairobi, Kenya, I visited a struggling family. After dinner the youngest child asked if I would like to meet the family pet. "Of course," I replied. He disappeared into the back room and came out with a huge smile on his face. I jumped up and stumbled to the back of the room. Resting in his hands was the largest, hairiest tarantula I've ever seen. This pet evoked dramatically different emotion in both of us; pleasure for him and fear for me.

The ancient Greek philosopher Epictetus argues that we are disturbed not by an object, but by the views we take of it. Is a tarantula an object of affection or a threat? It depends, argues Epictetus, on your point of view. Building on this observation, communication scholars have developed a theory called the "perceptual view of emotions," which asserts that our internal perceptions shape what external objects mean to us. Objects, events and people have no meaning until we attach meaning to them. Once we do, our perception evokes an emotional reaction. "Thus, our perceptions filter our experiences, and it is the filtered experiences that influence what we feel and how we respond," writes communication researcher Julia Wood.[7]

Here's an example. My wife and I had agreed to watch some friends' two small children so they could have a night out. While our guests were playing with our three young boys, a thunderstorm rolled in. Soon the night sky lit up with flashes of lightning and thunder boomed. The reaction from the kids couldn't have been more diverse. With each crack of thunder our visitors cried harder, wanting to go home, while our boys clapped and cheered. Why?

Ever since I can remember we had taught the boys that thunder was God bowling. Loud thunder was merely God rolling an applause-worthy strike! Each child had the same experience—hearing thunder—yet they had dramatically different emotions based on how they had been influenced growing up. A central part of the perceptual view of emotions is the idea that we all belong to emotional communities such as families, religious groups, schools, neighborhoods and organizations that provide experiences, perceptual filters and rules for what constitutes an appropriate emotion.

Our emotional communities provide us guidelines for emotions called "framing rules." A framing rule informs us of the emotional meaning of any given situation. My wife comes from a wonderful Irish family that has greatly influenced how she reacts to certain situations. For instance, when mourning the death of a relative, many Irish families hold both a wake and a funeral. A few days before the funeral, family, friends, and neighbors gather to eat, reminisce, sing and share favorite stories of the departed. This celebration often occurs with the casket in the front of the room. Individuals operate under the framing rule that wakes are a time to celebrate and remember a life well lived. When the actual funeral occurs, a different framing rule requires that survivors show concern for those left behind and pay respect to the deceased. In conjunction with framing rules are "feeling rules," which, Wood continues, "tell us what we have a right to feel or what we are expected to feel in particular situations."[8] At an Irish wake, family members have the right to feel cheerful even though there has been a death in the family, while at a formal funeral service individuals are expected to feel grief and sadness.

Framing and feeling rules play a significant role in how we approach conflict on an emotional level. Say you're heading off to work when your teenage daughter comes to breakfast wearing an outfit that you deem inappropriate for school. Your framing rule tells you that in this situation you have every right to be disappointed and angry at her decision to violate the dress code you've instituted. If she were attending college and merely home visiting, the situation and framing rule would change. Because she is still in high school living in your house (framing rule), it is reasonable for you to be upset (feeling rule). This conviction that a child living under your roof needs to abide by your rules has been cultivated within an emotional community (your parents), who believed disrespect by children should engender appropriate anger and discipline. In contrast, your daughter feels that since she is a senior in high school and soon heading to college (framing rule), it is reasonable to be upset with an overly restrictive parent (feeling rule). An emotional community made up of like-minded friends buttresses her frustration and desire for independence.

When entering conflict it is crucial to take time to understand the framing and feeling rules we're operating under and the emotional community that has fostered them.[9] While understanding the origin of these rules will not resolve all differences, it can help give perspective and diffuse emotion, allowing you to offer a more measured and understanding response.

PREPARING TO ENGAGE

When the time comes to engage another person in a difficult conversation, what are the steps we can take to identify and express emotions? The following are some suggestions.

Take a read of your current emotional state. Like the audience member who shouted, "You lie!" to President Obama, we're all susceptible to having our emotions get the better of us. Foundational to expressing emotions effectively is recognizing the feelings we're experiencing before the conversation even starts. I say "feelings" because in most situations we experience multiple emotions.

For example, say your superior walks into your office and tells you that the report you've been working on for weeks needs to be rewritten. After that emotional bombshell, she simply turns and leaves. What wide range of emotions would you feel? Perhaps you would be embarrassed that your first draft didn't meet her standards. Maybe you'd feel anger at the abrupt way she dismissed weeks of work. Because you respect her and want to have a good working relationship, you may also feel sadness. There may even be fear that your promotion could now be at risk. The mistake we often make in situations like this is isolating and communicating only one emotion. Studies show that we usually focus on and communicate the most negative emotion of all those we experience.[10] If I communicate only my anger toward my supervisor and ignore my feelings of sadness fostered by my respect for her, the tone of the conversation can easily turn negative.

The first step in assessing your emotional state is to give words to your feelings. The difficulty is that many of us have poor emotional vocabularies. If we are angry, we simply say, "I'm mad!" Relying on "a small vocabulary of feelings is as limiting as using only a few terms to describe colors," write communication scholars Ronald Adler, Lawrence Rosenfeld and Russell Proctor. "To say that the ocean in all its moods, the sky as it varies day to day, and the color of your true love's eyes are all 'blue' only tells a fraction of the story."[11] In the situation with your supervisor, how mad are you? Are you irate or upset? Are you testy or indignant? When I counsel couples I ask them to provide at least three distinct descriptors for a single emotion. If a person tells me he or she is discouraged about the relationship, I ask him or her to provide additional words. There is a significant difference between feeling disheartened and feeling disappointed. A person can feel good about the overall relationship but still feel disappointed about one particular aspect. Conversely, a person who is disheartened may view the entire relationship as hopeless. The key is to reflect on and clarify your emotional state.

And surprisingly, a little reflection goes a long way. Psychologists Chad Burton and Laura King discovered that setting aside two days a week to reflect on one's emotional outlook for just two minutes brought about significant physical and psychological benefits. After six weeks of minimal reflection about their emotional reactions to persons, traumas and events, participants felt more settled and in control. The researchers describe this process as the "two-minute miracle."[12]

The second step in assessing our emotional state is to consider the potential volatility of our emotions and our ability to control them. Communication experts Roger Fisher and Daniel Shapiro suggest asking oneself three questions:

1. Are my emotions out of control? If we had the conversation now, do I know I'd say something I would later regret?

2. Are my emotions risky? Are powerful emotions simmering, raising the possibility that if the conversation gets heated, I won't be able to control them? "If you are finding it hard to concentrate on anything other than your emotions," state Fisher and Shapiro, "your emotional temperature is at least risky."[13]

3. Are my emotions manageable? Am I aware of my emotions and do I feel I can control them even if the conversation gets tense?

The ancient writers of the book of Proverbs admonish us to guard our lips so we will not speak rashly and come to ruin (Prov 13:3).

Understanding our emotional state is crucial in assessing whether we can at this moment effectively guard and control our speech.

Be aware of emotional contagion. In addition to guarding our speech, understanding our emotional state before entering a conversation is key because our emotions will be passed onto the other person and vice versa. This transfer of emotions is called "emotional contagion." "We catch feelings from one another as though they were some kind of virus," notes behavioral scientist Daniel Goleman.[14] In one study, participants took a survey assessing their emotional mood and level of emotional expressiveness. Researchers specifically paired a self-identified low-expressive individual with a high-expressive individual. After the survey, the pair spent two minutes alone in a room and were not allowed to speak to each other. At the end of the two minutes a researcher came in and asked them to take the same survey again. Each time, the less emotionally expressive person took on, in some degree, the emotions of the more expressive person just by being in the same room.[15] How can this transfer of emotions happen so quickly?

Behavioral experts like Goleman explain that our complex brains have a low and high road when taking in information such as emotions. The high road is the part of our brain that is keenly aware of facts and analyzes them accordingly. The low road is "circuitry that operates beneath our awareness, automatically and effortlessly, with immense speed."[16] While the high road allows us to think about the data we're receiving, the low road lets us feel before we're even aware of it. When we sense the sarcasm in a remark, "we have the low road to thank," Goleman says.[17]

In the last chapter we noted that nonverbal communication is always present in our interactions, making it impossible to not communicate. The same is true of emotions. We cannot avoid emotional contagion and the transfer of our emotions because our low road is always subconsciously taking in information and responding accordingly. This makes assessing our emotions before a difficult conversation crucial. Before every conversation we must recognize and manage our emotions, knowing that they will to some degree be transferred to the other person.

Use fractionation. This odd-sounding technique is a staple for experts at the Harvard Negotiation Project and is considered the most effective way of reducing the intensity of emotion during conflict. Fractionation is the process of breaking conflict down into smaller, more manageable portions. The idea is that the smaller the conflict, the less severe the emotion. For example, statements like "I feel unappreciated in this relationship!" or "Our communication climate is lousy" are too broad and emotionally charged. How can these feelings be broken down into a more manageable size without trivializing them?

The key is to use the simple x-y-z formula: when you do x, in situation y, I feel z. For example, a coworker feels that you are not respecting his religion and has grown increasingly defensive. Not respecting another person's faith tradition is a serious issue, but it is too broad to negotiate. It may be helpful to ask, "What causes you to feel disrespected?" Your coworker responds, "When you ask me about my religion, you tend to only point out what's wrong with it. You never try to find areas of agreement. So, what's the point of even asking me about my faith?" Putting his concerns into the x-y-z formula would read like this: When you only find faults (x) when I am describing my faith (y) it makes me feel belittled and defensive (z). While this method doesn't suggest a resolution, it helps both parties understand the source of the emotion. The x-y-z approach has "the advantage of clarifying the issue of concern for the recipient of strong emotion and urging the sender to take responsibility for his or her emotional reaction," write communication scholars William Wilmot and Joyce Hocker.[18]

After listening to your coworker's complaint, you might summarize the difficulty as follows: "What seems to be causing our emotions to escalate is that you view my challenges to your faith as being disrespectful, rather than how I intend them, as healthy debate." This formula can move individuals away from emotions to a discussion about how to address issues of faith. Communication scholars call this meta-communication—communication about our communication. For example, you could ask, "Would it be helpful if I didn't interrupt while you're describing aspects of your faith?" "Might it be more productive to start with areas of agreement rather than areas of disagreement?" "How can we structure our conversation so it comes across as healthy debate and not an attack that evokes strong emotions?"

CONCLUSION

While these suggestions focused on managing emotions are valuable, they contain an inherent flaw. In order to clarify and manage emotions we need to be disciplined and aware of our fluctuating emotional state. Success is determined by our emotional intelligence and skill.

The apostle Paul takes a fundamentally different approach. When calling Christians in the church at Ephesus to put away powerful emotions such as rage, bitterness and anger and to form healthy relationships, he didn't tell them to work harder. Rather, he encouraged them to "be filled with the Spirit" (Eph 5:18). What sets apart Christian communicators is their reliance on a spiritual power outside of them. How can that power be appropriated to manage emotions, address the antecedents of conflict, and bring healing to fractured relationships? We'll explore Paul's call to spiritual power and discipline in the next chapter.

SUMMARY

Managing emotions is crucial when engaging others. Keep these points in mind:

Misconception

Emotions are unpredictable and will undermine our ability to objectively and dispassionately discuss an issue; therefore emotions should be suppressed.

God and emotions

God has deep emotions in which he feels frustration, anger and delight.

Jesus exhibits a keen intellect and vibrant emotions such as surprise, joy, sorrow, grief, amazement, indignation and so on.

In our desire to be effective communicators we must embrace and express our emotions in ways that mirror and honor Christ.

Perception and emotions

The perceptual view of emotions asserts that our internal perceptions shape what external objects mean to us.

A framing rule informs us of the emotional meaning of any given situation.

A feeling rule tells us what we have a right to feel or what we are expected to feel in a particular situation.

Preparing to engage

Take a read of your current emotional state.

Assess the potential volatility of your emotions and your ability to control them. Are your emotions out of control? Are your emotions risky? Are your emotions manageable?

Be aware of emotional contagion and understand that the emotions you are experiencing before a conversation will be passed on to the other person.

Practice fractionation where conflict is broken down into smaller, more manageable portions.

Utilize the x-y-z formula: when you do x, in situation y, I feel z.

Spiritual Disciplines

Power to Resolve Conflict

If you fly regularly, you know there are many reasons a flight can be delayed. Overbooking, inclement weather and mechanical issues are common culprits. But the passengers of an American Eagle flight departing from New York to Washington experienced a four-hour delay due to something unexpected: a shouting match between flight attendants. What triggered the altercation? While instructing passengers to turn off all electronics—including cell phones—one attendant noticed the attendant in the back talking on her cell. That did it.

"Every cell phone must be off, now!" she said in a terse tone. "Including the attendant in the back!" The argument that ensued became so heated the cockpit was alerted and the plane had to turn back to the gate.

"I find it hard to believe the flight attendants couldn't work with each other for an hour," noted a frustrated passenger.[1]

Even though these two airline employees knew everyone was watching and that a confrontation could jeopardize their careers and the safety of passengers, they just couldn't stop themselves. What's more, each was a seasoned professional who had received extensive training in how to handle difficult people and situations. Apparently, though, in the heat of the moment, none of it mattered. While these women clearly understood the inappropriateness of their actions, when the verbal blows started they lacked perspective and the ability to stop.

Former heavyweight champion Mike Tyson once observed that everyone has a plan until he gets hit in the face. This is the inherent flaw in much of the current theorizing on conflict resolution: any strategy to resolve conflict usually gets abandoned once the conversation becomes heated. We've all had the experience of leaving a conversation only to regret how we acted or what we said. Social media adds to this problem—shooting off angry texts, tweets or emails is easy and often disastrous.

"Flaming" is a term used by social media scholars to describe emails or text messages sent in a rage. Flaming often includes profanity, all capital letters, and excessive exclamation points or question marks: "Do you KNOW what I'm TALKING ABOUT?!?!" Long before social media or out-of-control flight attendants existed, Jewish wisdom writers observed that like a "city whose walls are broken through is a person who lacks self-control" (Prov 25:28). This chapter addresses a pressing issue: how can we cultivate and utilize self-control during intense exchanges?

CULTIVATING SELF-CONTROL

The need for self-control is clear in the Scriptures' prescription for how to respond to those who frustrate or anger us. When cursed we are to pray for and bless those who mistreat us (Lk 6:28). While a fool shows his or her "annoyance at once," the prudent "overlook an insult" (Prov 12:16). The words from a wise person's mouth are consistently "gracious" (Eccles 10:12). The apostle Paul tells us that even when someone is undeniably in the wrong, those of us who are spiritual should seek to "restore that person gently" (Gal 6:1). Such commands seem not only wildly counterintuitive but unrealistic.

How can we adopt such a challenging communication style? How much self-control will it take to not only overlook an insult but also be gracious? How much personal transformation is needed to become the kind of person who meets insult with blessing? Christian author and theologian A. W. Tozer argues that the issue of self-control is what fundamentally separates Christian from non-Christian communicators. The non-Christian may desire to be gracious but looks inwardly for the ability to do so. "Somewhere there is a reservoir of moral power; if he [the non-Christian] can only get that awake somehow, if he can tune into it, if he can plug into his possibilities, he will be a wonderful fellow."[2] Tozer suggests that looking inward for moral power is flawed and not worthy of a follower of Christ: "We go beyond that; we go deeper than that. Jesus says, 'Ye shall receive power'—a potent force from another world, invading your life by your consent, getting to the roots of your life and transforming you into His kindness."[3]

This idea of an external transformative power is what separates Christ's teaching from that of other noted thinkers. Plato argued that if we know the good, we will want to be good. Aristotle taught that if we practice the good, we will be good. Each perspective, while worthy of consideration, has key deficiencies. I can know that eating healthy is good for me but still fail to do it. I can practice being patient and still succumb to shouting at you when we disagree.[4] In contrast, Jesus argued that knowing the good and even practicing it are not enough—we must have an infusion of goodness given to us.

This infusion is not some abstract dose of goodness but an intimate relationship with God's Spirit, who indwells each believer. The Scriptures paint a robust picture of the Holy Spirit in which we learn that the Spirit has an intellect (1 Cor 2:10), experiences emotions (Eph 4:30), makes decisions (Acts 16:6) and loves deeply (Rom 15:30). With our cooperation, the Spirit empowers us to do crucial things that will enhance our communication. The Spirit gives us power to grow in our relationship with God and others (Jn 14:16).

He helps us forgive those we feel have mistreated us (Eph 4:30, 32). And most importantly, he helps us consistently treat others in a way that is kind, gentle, good and peaceful (Gal 5:22-23).

Does this mean that if I'm a follower of Christ I will automatically receive this infusion of power when in need? Or do I share a responsibility to become a receptor of the Spirit's grace and power? If so, how do I connect with the Spirit as I pursue others?

SPIRITUAL DISCIPLINES

In his advice to a young Christian leader, the apostle Paul writes, "Train yourself to be godly" (1 Tim 4:7). The word "train" comes from the Greek word *gumnasia* from which we get our English words "gymnasium" and "gymnastics." The King James Bible translates *gumnasia* into the word "exercise," while the New American Standard opts for the word "discipline." What Paul is telling Timothy to do is begin to exercise or discipline himself in his pursuit of God and the lifestyle he has called us to embrace. The difficulty is that, for many of us, the idea of discipline has fallen out of favor. David Whitney, an author who studies spiritual discipline, writes that many Christians he meets are "a mile wide and an inch deep. There are no deep, time-worn channels of communing discipline between them and God. They have dabbled in everything but disciplined themselves in nothing."[5]

These time-worn channels of communion with God are commonly referred to as spiritual disciplines, which Whitney defines as "personal and corporate disciplines that promote spiritual growth. They are habits of devotion and experiential Christianity that have been practiced by the people of God since biblical times."[6] These habits of thought and action can shape our character and infuse us with God's grace and power. Many Christians are uncomfortable with thinking of their spirituality as a discipline or habit. But if we consider the life of Christ, we observe him regularly taking time out of ministry to engage in spiritual practices such as fasting, prayer, meditation, worship and solitude, Matthew tells us Jesus would often remove himself from the crowds and spend the entire day alone in solitude and prayer (Mt 14:23).

These disciplines or habits were central to a rhythm of ministry cultivated by Christ. He would go off to engage God through habits of solitude and prayer, then return to engage the crowds with a sense of renewal. This pattern was not lost on a young German theologian, Dietrich Bonhoeffer, who argued that before you can be a part of a Christian community—filled with interpersonal tension and conflict—you must first be alone with God. "If you refuse to be alone you are rejecting Christ's call to you, and you can have no part in the community of those who are called," Bonhoeffer writes.[7] Foundational to living in harmony with others is the cultivation of spiritual habits that make community possible.

SPIRITUAL HABITS

A habit is "an ingrained tendency to act, think, or feel a certain way without needing to choose to do so."[8] A good friend of mine is a highly regarded surgeon whose specialty sometimes requires him to perform complex surgeries on infants. Each operation starts with the realization that if he makes one mistake and the surgery goes awry, his frail patient will die. His wife told me that after thirty years of experience and thousands of patients, she still wakes in the middle of the night to catch him practicing complex surgical techniques while sound asleep. These lifesaving procedures have become second nature to him. Before he enters the operating room he has already developed and honed habits.

"The star performer didn't achieve his excellence by trying to behave a certain way only during the game," notes philosopher Dallas Willard. "Instead he chose an overall life of preparation of mind and body, pouring all his energies into that total preparation, to provide a foundation in the body's automatic responses and strength for his conscious efforts during the game."[9] It is just as ridiculous for a baseball player to think he can hit a ninety-mile-an-hour fastball with no practice for a Christian to think she can respond to an insult with a blessing in the midst of a heated disagreement with no advance preparation. "Our mistake is to think that following Jesus consists in loving our enemies, going the 'second mile,' turning the other cheek, suffering patiently and hopefully—while living the rest of our lives just as anyone else," Willard writes.[10]

Willard is not advocating the adoption of a series of techniques but engaging in a lifestyle of pursuing God and his resources. Spiritual formation is not simply behavior modification but transformation of the mind, will and emotions. Merely labeling yourself a Christian or follower of Christ gives you as little power as dressing like a superhero would.

This is the hard lesson Benjamin Fedor learned in his attempt to curb crime in his neighborhood. Fedor, a self-described superhero who calls himself Phoenix Jones, patrols the streets of Seattle wearing a black mask and full-body muscle suit. He's not alone. The website reallifesuperheroes.com boasts nearly seven hundred members worldwide who dress as superheroes in order to take on lawbreakers. The difficulty individuals like Fedor have discovered is that the costume does not shield the wearer from injury or prosecution. Fedor has sustained multiple physical injuries and is currently facing assault charges in Seattle for spraying a crowd with pepper spray.[11] In the end, his costume gives him a false sense of security. This same false sense is found in self-professed Christians who cloak themselves with the label but do not embrace a holistic pursuit of Christ.

Marriage researcher Glenn Stanton notes that there is little substance to the claim that Christians divorce at roughly the same rate as non-Christians. While he concedes that those who merely identify themselves as Christian are just as susceptible to failed marriages as the general population, he argues that committed believers divorce radically less. He concludes:

Saying you believe something or merely belonging to a church, unsurprisingly, does little for marriage. But the more you are involved in the actual practice of your faith in real ways—through submitting yourself to a serious body of believers, learning regularly from Scripture, being in communion with God through prayer individually and with your spouse and children, and having friends and family around you who challenge you to take marriage seriously— the greater difference this makes in both the equality and longevity of our marriages.[12]

If we are serious about wanting to be gracious and Christ-honoring communicators who can exhibit self-control, we must fully commit to a way of life that includes spiritual discipline, reliance on God's power and the cultivation of godly habits. In order to see how these spiritual disciplines can help us prepare for difficult conversations, we'll consider what communication scholars identify as the area most disruptive to effective communication.

INTRAPERSONAL PERCEPTION

When we engage in conversations about passionate issues, two things often occur that make productive communication difficult. First, as we perceive the other person exhibiting communication behaviors that we deem uncivil or dishonest, our view of them and the relationship spirals downward. Second, we gradually absolve ourself of blame. It's the other person who has the problem or has contributed most to the conflict. The internal dialogue we have with ourself during a conversation is called "intrapersonal communication" and it can have a profoundly positive or negative influence on the conversation. So much so that conflict scholars William Wilmot and Joyce Hocker conclude that "intrapersonal perceptions are the bedrock upon which conflict are built."[13]

The power of intrapersonal perception became obvious during a conflict workshop I facilitated. To start, I asked participants to describe a conflict—as objectively as they could—from their perspective. Here is a sampling of responses:

"This person never reaches out to me!"

"My dad doesn't care about me."

"All she wants in our friendship is someone to tell her how great she is!"

"I have never felt acknowledged in my family."

"My coworker will never change!"

Notice how dogmatic and negative the perceptions are in these views. Imagine trying to resolve an issue with a coworker you perceive will never change or seeking to reconcile with a parent you think doesn't care about you. Unless this negative perception is addressed, no amount of communication strategies will help. The first step in creating healthy dialogue is to address our inner talk and perceptions through the spiritual disciplines.

SOLITUDE

Many who study the spiritual disciplines argue that the practice of solitude is the most fundamental discipline. It is the decision to abstain from speaking or exposing ourselves to outside noise or stimulus in order to open us to Spirit-led introspection. In order to change how we view ourselves and others, we must allow the Spirit not only to bring our perspective to light, but also to challenge it. "Search me, O God," declares David, "and know my heart; test me and know my anxious thoughts" (Ps 139:23). The difficulty is that in today's techno-savvy world we have developed an aversion to silence. To combat this we must intentionally carve out times to listen to the promptings and insights of the Spirit. This can happen in a multitude of ways:

Create pockets of solitude. In our fast-paced, social media–saturated world, spending a day or afternoon alone is difficult. However, get into the habit of cultivating pockets of solitude throughout the day. Some of my students tell me that the first thing they do in the morning—before getting out of bed or going to the bathroom—is to check texts, emails or Facebook. Before you jump into this technological riptide, take a minute or two to be silent. Turn off the radio or cell phone during your commute to work or class and tune in to God's perspective.

Create an environment of solitude. When is it the most quiet in your house or apartment? Early in the morning or late at night? During the week, select a few days to set the alarm twenty minutes early to have the downstairs to yourself before the mad rush of getting out the door begins. If morning doesn't work, leave the Nano and cell at home and go for a late walk alone.

Practice a market day of the soul. The Puritans understood the need for regular times of solitude and rest, calling Sunday the "market day of the soul." What they understood that modern believers do not is the role the soul plays in keeping our selfishness in check and providing grace to resolve conflict. In this light, the sabbath is the deliberate cultivation of a spiritual reservoir. Just as a marathon runner loads up on enough carbohydrates to last the entire race, we need to prepare for the challenges of the upcoming week. Taking one day or a half a day a week to tune out social media, avoid distractions and be still before God is essential.

Be warned: setting out to create these times of solitude is challenging. In the conflict workshop I mentioned earlier, participants were asked to cultivate seven pockets of solitude during the weekend and spend one afternoon alone in silence. Simply put, most failed. Here are some responses:

> "I am really appalled and frightened at my lack of discipline when it comes to using my phone. It has become so ingrained that throughout the day I text whenever I want. When I do get the chance to be alone I search people out, possibly in fear of being alone."

"Facebook is really hard for me to cut out. I have a routine that consists of waking up each morning and checking my Facebook and email. I feel addicted to Facebook."

"It was honestly so hard for me to not listen to music on the drive here. Every time I got in the car and drove in silence I felt uncomfortable."

"I feel that each moment has to be occupied."

"It was really difficult for me to sit in silence. I realize that I use every minute of my time to get something done."

As we carve out times of silence and solitude, we need to focus on two things. First, we need to ask God for insight into the conflict we are facing. As we seek to resolve disagreements with others, are we behaving in a way that God would find pleasing? Are we extending grace to those who disagree with us? What role do we play in this conflict? Do we regularly meet an insult with an insult? What keeps us from offering a blessing instead? Are we speaking more truth than love? Taking time to allow the Spirit to answer these questions is crucial. "To simply refrain from talking, without listening to God, is not silence," says author Richard Foster.[14]

Second, we need to become aware of our own internal dialogue and check negative thoughts about a person. For solitude to be effective we must, as the apostle Paul suggests, learn to take captive our thoughts (2 Cor 10:5). Paul is using a military metaphor where soldiers identify an enemy, subdue him and take him captive. If my times of solitude are invaded by negative thoughts about another person, then I will be distracted and preoccupied rather than quiet. Recently I learned how hard managing thoughts can be. While we have three boys who play sports, my wife and I have been able to stay out of the ugly politics often associated with organized sports. That is, until last year.

A group of angry parents accused one of our boy's coaches of verbally abusing players and brought the issue before the school

board. We knew the coach and thought the claims completely unfounded. I was asked to speak to before the school board and give
my opinion. The room was packed mostly with parents who supported the coach, except for an angry and determined minority. I
carefully defined verbal abuse from an academic perspective and
stated that in all the years I'd known him I'd never seen him be
abusive in games or at practice. After the meeting we were shocked
by the response from those who disagreed. My family and I became
targets in chat rooms, on electronic bulletin boards and on
Facebook. Some even called into question my faith by asking how
a so-called Christian could defend a man who abused kids.

I was hurt and angry. I knew I needed to be alone with God to
gain perspective, but it proved difficult. Every time I attempted to
be silent before the Lord, my mind would race toward negative
thoughts about individuals. For a time I went to bed and woke up
thinking about them. My attempts at solitude were futile. C. S.
Lewis argues that for many of us the worries or struggles of life
come rushing at us "like wild animals." Our job, suggests Lewis,
"consists in shoving them all back" and opening ourselves to God's
voice.[15] But how? How do we shove back the negative thoughts
toward others as we attempt to be still before God?

During this time of personal attack I came across an ancient
prayer adopted by the early church. This prayer, referred to as the
Jesus Prayer, is derived from the Gospel of Luke where in humility a tax collector prays, "God, have mercy on me, a sinner"
(Lk 18:13). This simple prayer was adopted by the ancient church
and expanded to "Lord Jesus Christ, Son of God, have mercy on
me, a sinner." Throughout church history God has used this
prayer in remarkable ways in the lives of countless believers. I
have found it crucial in learning to manage my own intrapersonal
communication. When I spend time with God in solitude and
begin to entertain negative thoughts, I counter with, "Lord Jesus,
have mercy on me!"

This phrase is not only a prayer but a way of controlling my self-talk. Once these negative thoughts have been blunted, I remind myself of things I know to be true of the other person. He or she is loved by God. Just as God's Spirit is working on me I can be assured that the Spirit is equally convicting him or her. And the person with whom I'm in conflict faces pressures and struggles unknown to me.

How many times should we utilize this prayer? We can use it to counter each negative thought that is pervading our intrapersonal perception and inhibiting solitude.[16] After a while, the Jesus Prayer can be replaced or augmented with Scripture. If we feel a pervasive lack of peace concerning a relationship or conflict it may be helpful to pray through Paul's prescription for anxiety when unsettling thoughts come: "Do not be anxious about anything, but in every situation, by prayer and petition, with thanksgiving, present your requests to God" (Phil 4:6).

CONFESSION

Engaging in solitude naturally leads to times of confession. Confession, notes Christian author Adele Calhoun, "means we open the bad in our lives to God. We invite him to come right in and look at our sin with us. We don't hide by being good, moral people or in neurotic self-recriminations."[17] As mentioned earlier, a key pitfall of intrapersonal perception is that it often leads to our slowly absolving ourselves from blame in conflict.

In times of solitude we hold ourselves up to the biblical standard and ask God to show us how we fare in our interactions with others. For example, in admonishing believers to live in unity, Peter lays out his expectation for the church. "Finally, all of you, be like-minded, be sympathetic, love one another, be compassionate and humble. Do not repay evil with evil or insult with insult. On the contrary, repay evil with blessing" (1 Pet 3:8-9). Peter's admonition serves as a checklist in our interaction with others. When disagreeing with a person, am I sympathetic to his or her perspective?

For instance, if I were convinced that a coach was being abusive to my child, how passionate and forceful would I be in defending him or her? Even if I disagree with a person, is my communication loving, compassionate and humble, or do I come across as hateful, hardhearted and arrogant? Do I quickly meet an insult with an insult, or can I offer a blessing to those who forcefully oppose me? The word "bless" is translated from *eulgontes,* which literally means to speak well of someone. Times of confession allow me to evaluate my actions according to a standard set by the Scriptures rather than by those around me.

WORSHIP

After speaking at marriage conferences for more than sixteen years I've discovered that what is missing for couples who struggle deeply is a belief that things can improve. This discouragement isn't limited to marriage. Remember the participant in my workshop who wrote in his assessment that he believed his boss would never change? If you keep telling yourself a person is incapable of change, then why even try? While it is prudent to realize that we are limited in how much we can fundamentally alter a spouse, child or coworker, we must remember that God is not limited.

"Now to him who is able to do immeasurably more than all we ask or imagine, according to his power that is at work within us," Paul prays for the church at Ephesus (Eph 3:20). While most of us are familiar with Paul's prayer, we often overlook the context. Paul was praying for a church made up of diverse individuals consisting of Jews and Gentiles, rich and poor, slaves and masters, and men and women who were linked by their common faith but came from wildly different backgrounds and frames of reference. At times these differences caused strife and disagreement. Paul gives the church hope by reminding them God can unify them in ways that seem unimaginable.

Worship is the act of redirecting our focus toward God and acknowledging who he is and what he can do. "Worship is the God-centered focus and response of the inner man; it is being preoccupied with God," writes Donald Whitney.[18] Perhaps the reason Paul offered his prayer with such conviction is that he never forgot his own transformation. Before his unlikely conversion, Paul—then known as Saul of Tarsus—persecuted the early church. He describes his pre-conversion life as being motivated by religious zeal and being obsessed with persecuting "the church of God" and trying to "destroy it" (Gal 1:13). Not only did Paul stand by and watch the stoning of the early church leader Stephen, he gave his "approval to his death" (Acts 8:1).

Yet he changed. While traveling from Jerusalem to Damascus to arrest and interrogate followers of Christ, Paul unexpectedly encountered the resurrected Christ (Acts 9:3-9). It was an experience that forever changed the trajectory of his life. Who could have anticipated the radical conversion that led him to become the gospel's most ardent messenger and leader of the New Testament church? Of the twenty-seven books in the New Testament Paul is credited with writing thirteen. His influence continues to shape the church worldwide. If your intrapersonal perception is laced with the idea that people cannot change, then reshaping your focus by worshiping God is crucial.

By encouraging you to worship God I'm not limiting you to corporate worship within the confines of a building or during one day of the week. "If you will not worship God seven days a week," notes Tozer, "you do not worship Him one day a week."[19] Worship, then, is cultivating the habit of regularly focusing on God and allowing a biblical view of him to shape our self-talk and expectations of what is possible. To expand your view of God, consider these passages: Psalm 139, Isaiah 6, and Job 38–42.

THE IMPORTANCE OF POSTURE

As modern Christians we have sorely neglected the role of the body in our spiritual lives. We think the position of the body has little to do with anything, and so when practicing the discipline of worship or prayer we fail to engage our bodies. But if I'm praying about a particular conflict, my posture needs to reflect what I'm doing— communicating with God. This past year I've made the decision to pray standing up with arms raised. My decision to pray with arms raised is motivated by Paul's instruction to Timothy that believers should intercede for others by "lifting up holy hands" (1 Tim 2:8).

This decision came about after I again watched the end of the 1962 classic *To Kill a Mockingbird*. Atticus Finch (played by Gregory Peck) is a Depression-era attorney defending a black man accused of rape in the then racist South. To no one's surprise, an all-white jury convicts. As a dejected Finch leaves the courthouse, a group of African Americans stands as he passes. Everyone stands silently except Finch's daughter, who remains seated. An elderly black man leans over and whispers to the girl, "Stand up, Jean Louise. Your father is passing by." They stood in awe of Finch's courage and dignity.

Does God deserve any less? I decided to stand while praying as recognition of my awe toward a righteous and powerful God. Does God hear me any better by my standing with arms raised? No. But I become more attentive to what I am doing. I find that standing with arms raised helps me to be mindful that I'm communicating with a God who deserves my attention and respect.

DURING THE CONVERSATION

Once we find ourselves in the midst of a tense conversation, our self-talk will need to be closely monitored. If we encounter accusations or sarcasm, no doubt our intrapersonal perceptions will turn negative, which if unchecked will sabotage the conversation. We need to fall back on the habit of countering each thought, as soon as it materializes, with prayer. This can take the form of the Jesus Prayer or passages we've memorized in advance. One passage I like to dwell on during a difficult conversation is Paul's admonition: "You who live by the Spirit should restore that person gently" (Gal 6:1).

This verse reminds me of two key questions to ask during the conversation: Am I relying on the Spirit's power and leading? Am I correcting this person gently as I disagree?

If during the conversation I start to tell myself that this person is beyond hope or we'll never find resolution, I need to continue the habit of worship where I focus on God's ability to move hearts. God's power is so vast that not even a king's heart is beyond his reach: "The king's heart is like channels of water in the hand of the LORD; He turns it wherever He wishes" (Prov 21:1 NASB). Often God will use us—as we communicate grace and compassion and offer blessing instead of insult—to touch the hearts of those with whom we disagree. If during the conversation we withhold grace, are hard-hearted, or match insult with insult, we need to immediately practice the habit of confession and move on.

During the entire interaction we'll be having multiple conversations. As we speak to the other person we'll also be speaking to ourselves addressing our self-talk and speaking to God asking that he give us power to do what the Spirit leads us to do.[20] As we engage in a difficult conversation we can be assured that God is present and active. The prophet Nehemiah not only acknowledges God's presence but speaks to him as he addresses King Artaxerxes: "The king said to me, 'What is it you want?' Then I prayed to the God of heaven, and I answered the king" (Neh 2:4-5).[21] Like Nehemiah, we would be wise to talk to God as we talk to others.

Preparing to enter into a difficult conversation forces us to ask what type of communicator we are. Do we seek to muster up compassion, patience and self-control by looking inward, or do we focus on God and his resources? Is our confidence in ourselves or God? Is God worthy of my trust?

CONCLUSION

Researchers at Stanford University are discovering the mental benefits of reclaiming a sense of awe. After watching videos of whales jumping out of the ocean or a panoramic view of the northern lights, study participants reported feeling awe accompanied by a sense of calm in which time seemed to stop. This resulted in an increased feeling of happiness. It seems that these awe-inspiring experiences powerfully—though temporarily—alter our perspective.[22]

To a Christian, worship is reclaiming a sense of awe by looking not merely at creation but focusing on the Creator. The Psalmist declares, "Be still and know I am God" (Ps 46:10). The spiritual disciplines "put us in a place where we can begin to notice God and respond to his word."[23] As we focus on God we'll develop habits that can change our perspective and how we communicate with others. In the next section we'll consider a strategy gleaned from the Scriptures that can, with God's assistance, help us have productive conversations with those who matter most.

SUMMARY

When preparing to have difficult conversations make sure to address these key areas.

Self-control

Remember Tozer's observation of where a Christian seeks the power to be self-controlled: "Jesus says, 'Ye shall receive power'—a potent force from another world, invading your life by your consent, getting to the roots of your life and transforming you into His kindness." Are we trying to muster up self-control from within? Or . are we attempting to cultivate self-control from God's power via the spiritual disciplines?

Self-talk

Intrapersonal perceptions are the bedrock for conflict. Make sure to monitor and address negative thoughts about a person before and during the conversation.

Spiritual disciplines

In order to address self-talk make sure to utilize the following disciplines:

- Solitude

- Prayer

- Confession

- Worship

Remember, Jesus regularly used these very habits as he sought to minister to others.

During the conversation

Utilize each discipline as needed during the conversation. Engage in prayer as negative thoughts materialize. Confess negative attitudes and move on. Focus on God when you are tempted to despair that things will never change in a relationship.

Awe therapy

The Psalmist says, "Be still and know that I am God" (Ps 46:10). The goal of the spiritual disciplines is to put us in a place where we can begin to notice God and respond to his Word before, during and after the conversation.

Organizing a Conversation

Most of us enter a conversation without a clear idea of how to organize it. What is the best way to start? Should I just start talking or ask her to begin? How quickly should I disagree with what he is saying? What do I hope to accomplish?

How we structure a conversation is crucial, and in the following chapters we'll consider a strategy for organizing a conversation. The strategy centers on four essential questions that we must ask during an encounter with someone from a markedly different perspective. Each question must be asked and answered in sequence. Once we feel we have the answer to one question, we can move on to the next.

As we consider these questions it may be helpful to work through a real-life situation that shows their value. While I was in graduate school I received a frantic call from parents who were deeply concerned about their son Mark. He was at the same institution finishing his PhD in religious studies and had abruptly informed them he no longer believed Christianity was true. Almost everything Mark had been raised to *believe about the Bible, Jesus and faith were now being tossed aside. It was every Christian parent's nightmare.*

They pleaded with me to meet with him to talk. Mark reluctantly agreed to grab coffee and we set a date. Heading into the conversation we both knew it could be awkward and perhaps contentious—he was abandoning his faith and I was the person hand-picked by his parents to talk him out of it. How do you organize such a difficult conversation? I determined to ask the four questions that you'll read about in the following chapters. The first step was to listen.

Question One

What Does This Person Believe?

One day a friend of mine, Jane, was driving home across a bridge she had crossed a hundred times. This time, she and her companion saw something so out of place that they almost didn't stop. There, standing on the edge of the bridge, was a beautiful, elderly woman. She was dressed in a fur coat wearing a bright, colorful hat. What made my friend stop was that she was standing on the outside of the rails leaning forward, poised to jump. While her friend frantically dialed 911 on her cell phone, Jane got out of the car and carefully approached. By now other cars had stopped. As she approached, Jane tried to remember scenes from movies where trained negotiators calmly talked down despondent individuals. None came to mind.

"My name is Jane. What's yours?" she said softly, her heart pounding.

There was no response. The only sound was wind rushing against both of them.

"You are a beautiful woman and you seem very sad." As she

spoke, Jane gestured to the crowd to stay back. The woman's eyes remained fixed on the dark water below.

"I would like to hear what has made you so sad," Jane said, now a few feet away from the woman. In slow motion, the woman turned her head and made eye contact.

"She didn't look frantic or desperate," Jane explained. "She just looked tired and lost." Then, just as suddenly as it started, the ordeal was over. With her eyes locked on Jane, the woman tentatively reached out a hand and was saved.

"I honestly didn't know what I was doing," Jane told me. "I just offered to listen. What else could I do?"

After hearing that story I've often wondered why it worked. How did two strangers form an immediate and lifesaving connection? "When we love another," notes psychologist M. Scott Peck, "we give him or her our attention."[1] By offering to listen to this desperate woman my friend, in fact, offered her love. The first step in our communication strategy is to suppress our desire to persuade or correct the person with whom we disagree, but rather to listen. The first question we need to answer is: What does this person believe? Communication scholars and the Scriptures stress the value of listening.

THE IMPORTANCE OF LISTENING

Most of us spend at least fifty percent of our waking time listening to those around us.[2] In the business world executives and managers report that sixty percent of their time is spent listening. In a study that asked participants to rate which communication skills were most important in both establishing a career and in interpersonal relationships, listening was ranked first in both categories.[3] Many scholars argue that listening is central to our well-being as humans. John Gentile, a scholar who focuses on storytelling as a form of healing, argues that "the acts of story, both storytelling and storylistening—of telling one's story, of listening to another person's story, or another person listening to our own—are fundamental to our humanity and sense of well-being."[4]

The idea that telling our story and listening to another person's story is central to our humanity led one activist to create something called a "listening booth." StoryCorps, the brainchild of Dave Isay, was launched on October 23, 2003, in New York's Grand Central Terminal. The concept is simple: you walk into the booth with someone whose story you want to hear. A facilitator meets you and seats both of you at a table with a microphone. The facilitator hits record and you get to ask that person questions that you've always wanted answered: "What are your greatest convictions?" "How do you want to be remembered?" "What is your advice about how to authentically love others?" Two CDs are created—one for you and one that becomes part of the archive at the American Folklife Center at the Library of Congress.

The response has been overwhelming. So many people have participated that Isay and his associates have opened another booth at Ground Zero in downtown Manhattan and have created portable booths that go out to the public. StoryCorps is based on two simple principles: First, if we take time to listen, we'll find wisdom, passion and even poetry in every person's narrative. Second, listening is an act of love.[5] "There is no agony," states listening scholar Jimmie Manning, "like bearing an untold story inside you."[6] One of the most important ways we can show love to another person is to take time to listen and unearth his or her stories.

The Scriptures also place a strong value on listening. The book of Proverbs presents listening as being vital to effective communication. Not only is the act of listening commended, but its primacy is stressed. "To answer before listening—that is folly and shame" (Prov 18:13). While we may understand why speaking before listening is folly—giving our opinion without first gathering the facts exposes us to many potential problems—it is interesting that the ancient writer would suggest that speaking before listening is shameful. To deem listening unnecessary is to communicate that the other person is inferior and that his or her perspective does not matter; all that matters in the conversation is what we have to say. A wise communicator understands it is better to silently "store up knowledge," while a fool talks prematurely and "invites ruin" (Prov 10:14). How is ruin avoided? By holding our tongue until the right moment (Prov 10:19).

In stark terms the ancient writers state that a fool takes no pleasure in understanding, but only in sharing his or her opinion (Prov 18:2), and that there is little hope for those of us who are hasty in our speech (Prov 29:20). While there is much to say about listening in the New Testament, the clearest endorsement is found when James argues that everyone should be "quick to listen, slow to speak and slow to become angry" (Jas 1:19). An old rabbinical saying observes that while God left the ears open and exposed for quick use, he walled the tongue in behind our teeth as a barrier against hasty use. In other words, God placed a speed bump to keep our tongue in check.

By choosing to make listening the first step in our communication strategy, we move from being potential adversaries in conversation to partners with a common goal, attending to the same perspective. This shift "gives you a chance to engage them in a cooperative task—that of understanding their problem," writes communication author William Ury. "And it makes them more willing to listen to you."[7]

OBSTACLES

However, while we may accept the importance of listening in theory, there are many obstacles to practicing it effectively.

Overassessment of skills. When I ask people if they have ever taken a class on listening, many scoff at the idea. "Why would you need a class on listening?" is the most common reply. Many of us underestimate the complexity of the process listening and overestimate our own proficiency. In one study, a group of managers were asked to rate their listening skills. No manager rated herself or himself as a "poor" or "very poor" listener. In fact, more than ninety percent placed themselves in the "good" or "very good" category. When employees were asked to rate the listening skills of these same managers, the most common response was "weak."[8]

If the first step to our communication strategy is to become a proficient listener, we must honestly evaluate our knowledge of listening strategies and our ability to enact these strategies. How would those around us describe us as a listener?

Prejudgment. A Baptist said of an Episcopalian, "I cannot hear you because of what I expect you to say." One difficulty with having recurring conversations with the same individual is that we start to think we know everything that person is about to say. Heading into the conversation, we are convinced we already know his or her position and we've already decided he or she is wrong. What new information could this person possibly offer? I've heard it all before and I simply don't agree. The first step of our strategy requires us to enter into a conversation with a fresh perspective. Even though we've discussed this issue many times, what new information can we uncover?

Long before C. S. Lewis became a famous Christian apologist he was a literary critic. He believed that the sure mark of an "unliterary" person was that he or she considered "I've read it already" to be "a conclusive argument against reading a work." Lewis believed that you simply could not get a deep understanding of a book by merely reading it once. "Those who read great works, on the other hand, will read the same work ten, twenty, or thirty times."[9] Certainly, the opinions of the person we disagree with are not on par with great literary works! We don't need to hear them multiple times to know he or she is misguided. Yet to that person, his or her views are complex and passionate and deserve to be attended to multiple times to fully understand and appreciate them. Remember, we listen not only to effectively gather facts and information, but also to convey love.

Being quick to react. "Human beings are reaction machines," writes Ury.[10] All of us have certain words or phrases that push our emotional buttons. Phrases such as "you never" or "you always" are emotionally charged and often force an immediate reaction that quickly sets aside listening. When we respond to emotionally charged language, we "give up our responsibility to think critically about what others say, to consider their words carefully instead of reacting unthinkingly to particular words," notes Julia Wood.[11]

"Whoever has understanding is even-tempered," suggest the Jewish wisdom writers (Prov 17:27). In the original Hebrew, the text literally states that a wise person is cool of spirit.[12] A key element of effective listening is to keep a cool composure and open mind while listening to ideas or accusations you feel are unfair or unfounded. No doubt the ability to do this will depend on having already cultivated spiritual discipline and habits long before the conversation starts.

Ambushing. Sometimes we enter a conversation simply with the goal of winning the argument. Ambushing involves gathering information that will later be used to attack the speaker. Far from not listening, ambushers are often very adept at listening and ask carefully designed questions that lead a person into a trap. They often fake interest to keep a person speaking or to lower his or her defenses. Listening and understanding are merely tools to an end. While ambushing can be effective in winning a debate, it is a strategy that usually only works once. After a person has been ambushed he or she usually adopts a defensive posture in the next conversation. A person who regularly ambushes others in conversation soon shreds his or her credibility. As already discussed in section one, our credibility or ethos is directly tied to our goodwill.

Are we sincerely trying to listen to others in order to understand, or are we using listening techniques to set a conversational trap? For example, a key component of the Christian worldview is a belief in absolute truth. We believe that truth is not relative or limited to a person's point of view. If something is true (God's existence, for example) then it is true for everyone, not just believers. A form of ambushing occurs when we ask the skeptic, "Do you believe truth is relative?" If the person answers, "Yes," we pounce! "How can you know your view is true if all truth is relative?" This "gotcha" moment may win an abstract philosophical point but communicates that winning the argument is more important than genuine understanding and dialogue.

Conversational narcissism. Narcissists are individuals who have an egotistical preoccupation with their own preferences, aspirations and sense of self. Communication is merely a means to express their ideas and dominate the talk stage. In such a communication style there is little desire to listen or focus on the views of others. The only opinion that matters is theirs.

To measure the prevalence of this kind of attitude, communication researcher Carl Trosset presented two hundred college students with a detailed list of personal and provocative topics such as whether race was "an important difference between people." Participants were then asked if they thought it was possible to have an open, give-and-take conversation about such sensitive topics. To Trosset's surprise, the vast majority of participants said they had no desire to engage another person's perspective on sensitive issues. They merely wanted to voice their opinion. Only five percent of the test group expressed a desire to understand and learn more about another person's view.[13]

Apparently, when it comes to provocative topics, it's easy to adopt a narcissistic communication style where our primary—or sometimes only—goal is to share our viewpoint. The Scriptures advocate a different orientation where we are not only to be "devoted to one another in love" but also "honor one another above yourselves" (Rom 12:10). Similarly, to be Christlike entails focusing not merely on our own interests but equally on the interests of others (Phil 2:4).

Message complexity. Listening is often laborious due to the complexity of people's messages. The reasons why people hold different positions or convictions are often confusing and disorganized. Sometimes it takes much effort and focus to follow a person's line of thought and sometimes we are simply not up for it. And message complexity is exacerbated by the constant overload of information streaming from social media and the Internet. Is it possible that we are gradually losing our ability to focus on complex messages? In his thoughtful essay "Is Google Making Us Stupid?" Nicholas Carr argues that we cope with the endless stream of electronic information by engaging in "power browsing," in which we bounce from site to site to skim through articles for quick hits of information. Carr is not alone. He quotes a researcher at the University of Michigan who candidly stated in his blog that he no longer has the attention span to read *War and Peace*—even "a blog post of more than three or four paragraphs is too much to absorb. I skim it."[14]

Sadly, we may also rely on power browsing to quickly sum up people. Last year I was asked to serve on a panel to comment on the art exhibit of a fellow faculty member. As usual, I was in a hurry the day of the panel and thought I could pop in to the exhibit and write down some thoughts to share that night. As I entered the hall I encountered the first painting. It was a richly textured canvas covered in white paint. That was it. The title placard simply read, "One." As I scanned the other paintings I realized that the entire exhibit was a collection of abstract art. The works were stunning in their appearance, but they offered no ready interpretation. I soon discovered that the beauty and deep frustration of abstract art is its refusal to offer easy interpretations. If you are not ready to seriously ponder a painting, then you should just leave. Power browsing simply isn't an option.

Many of the perspectives we encounter when debating complex issues will often resemble abstract art. The book of Proverbs acknowledges the complexity of human motives and states that the "purposes of a person's heart are deep waters, but one who has insight draws them out" (Prov 20:5). Old Testament scholar William McKane says this proverb suggests that understanding another person is like dropping a bucket into a person's heart, where opinion and intellectual judgments are made, and then drawing it back out.[15] Often these opinions are submersed in dark waters and will require a commitment to patiently bring them to the surface.

Gender differences. While men and women value listening equally, there are differences in how they approach the process. Unfortunately, these differences can impede listening. But if part of our goal is to acknowledge another person's perspective, we must listen in a way that makes him or her feel heard. For example, women are generally more active in their listening styles, tend to build on the ideas of others, and regularly invite others to be part of the conversation by nodding in agreement, maintaining eye contact and offering feedback. Gender scholar Pamela Fishman describes a feminine listening style as "maintenance work," because the goal is to maintain and foster communication. Maintenance work is primarily advanced through listening cues that invite elaboration, such as, "I often feel the same way" or "I would have done the same thing!" Many women will not feel heard if there is not regular feedback or participation by the other person.

However, individuals brought up in a masculine orientation generally are more protective of the talk stage and may view constant feedback as a challenge or lack of respect. Men often use communication in an instrumental sense to accomplish communicative goals. We are usually less emotionally expressive and offer only minimal listening cues such as "uh-huh" or "yeah." For many men, communication follows a sequence in which one person is allowed to speak uninterrupted while the other person listens with minimal distraction or participation. Once a man makes his point, a listener is allowed to assume the talk stage to either agree or disagree. If these different orientations are not acknowledged, it may cause problems.[16]

Early in our marriage, my wife and I struggled to adapt to each other's preferences. As she would speak, I would—out of respect to her—not interrupt. After a few minutes she stopped and said, "I feel like you're zoning out." I was surprised and told her I was listening and could recite back to her everything she had said. "I want you to engage me," was her response.

What I thought was focused listening didn't register with her. Instead of becoming defensive I needed to shift to her preferred style of listening. Knowing these different gender preferences are crucial to effective listening.

THE GOALS OF LISTENING

While there are many reasons to listen to others—for pleasure, to support someone, to gather information—two key reasons are to understand and evaluate. Even though both are important, the order in which they are done is crucial to establishing a productive conversation. Being too quick to evaluate a person's perspective or argument can produce defensiveness, and the communication climate can easily spiral downward. Each goal of listening deserves our attention.

Listening to evaluate. "The simple believe anything" (Prov 14:15). A crucial component of listening is to engage in critical listening, where we evaluate the claims, facts and recollection of past events offered by the speaker. Does his or her representation of past events square with events as remembered by others and myself? Is the argument logical? Are there contradictions that need to be addressed? Is there another perspective or version of the facts that the speaker is neglecting to consider?

During a difficult conversation, evaluation often means offering feedback that challenges the view of the speaker. But it is imperative that we not rush to hasty conclusions or too quickly contradict the person speaking. In fact, the central argument of this book is that evaluation is most effective if we cultivate understanding first. Our communication strategy brings about understanding through listening (step one), exploring reasons why beliefs have been adopted (step two) and cultivating common ground (step three). The evaluation stage is the fourth and last step of our model. First, we need to focus on what a person believes about issues that separate us.

Listening to understand. The first step in seeking to understand another person's view is to set aside our assumptions of what he or she will say and temporarily keep in check our own opinions. Paradoxically, notes author Os Guinness, the first step in answering or responding to a person is not to have an answer, "for the genuine answer counts only if we have genuinely listened first."[17] Listening to understand entails the following elements.

Desire to understand. Listening scholar David Johnson states that the single most important factor in listening effectively is not some technique but the desire to understand.[18] Do we really want to engage and understand the other person? Giving individuals the space to share their thoughts is what gender scholar Sonia Johnson calls "hearing into being." "When we are free to talk without threat of interruption, evaluation, and the pressure of time we move quickly past known territory out into the frontiers of our thought," she writes.[19] People are amazingly adept at detecting whether we are faking interest or desire to truly understand.

Clarifying questions. We need to avoid pretending to understand a person's perspective if we really don't. I call such an approach "pseudolistening," which is pretending to listen and be attentive while in reality we are distracted, bored or focused on what we want to say when it's our turn to speak. If a phrase, term or idea is not clear, ask for clarification. "When you say I'm intolerant of your view, what do you mean by 'intolerant'?" "I'm not sure I understand what you mean when you identify yourself as a skeptic to all things religious. Could you elaborate?" "When you say I get defensive when we discuss finances, could you describe what I do that gives you that impression?" What keeps these questions from becoming an interrogation is our tone and attitude. Are we asking genuine questions or trying to trap the speaker? Are we asking questions to garner answers we can use in an ambush? The goal of asking questions is to achieve listening fidelity, which is to receive and understand as closely as possible what the person is attempting to convey.

Summary statements. After a person has finished speaking and you've asked for clarification, offer summary statements of what you think you've just heard. These statements require that you paraphrase and put into your own words the narrative of the person speaking—for example, "So, if I hear what you are saying, you feel in certain situations that . . . " While offering summary statements and paraphrasing are often considered to be the core of effective listening, they can powerfully confirm or disconfirm the speaker. They will disconfirm if our paraphrase is factually inaccurate or if we get the facts straight but miss the emotional tone of the speaker.

I was once facilitating a discussion with a couple that was experiencing conflict. After the wife shared her feelings of being neglected, the husband paraphrased back her concerns. She showed no reaction. "I suppose he was listening," was her response to me. While the husband got the facts right, he missed the emotions that undergirded her frustration. I asked him to describe not what she thought but how she was feeling. Tears rolled down her face as he described how he thought his obsession with work must make her feel. Step one of our strategy requires that we keep summarizing a person's perspective until we get it not only in content and tone, but the person feels confirmed.

Perspective taking. Perspective taking is the attempt to see the world through the eyes of the other person. We temporarily set aside our own views to understand how a person views reality and us within his or her reality. For many people, air travel is the preferred way to travel. While it has its own set of risks, most believe that it is safer to fly than drive. Yet what if you had a fear of flying fueled by the belief that getting on a plane was unsafe and even life-threatening? If you had that perspective, for whatever reason, would you get on the plane? No. The problem is that we quickly evaluate the fear and find it unfounded or silly.

The same is true of our encounters with those who reject the Christian worldview because they think Christians are intolerant, homophobic, anti-intellectual and hypocritical. Would you join a community if you thought it were made up of members with those qualities? Of course not. But we rush to defend the Christian worldview without first considering the other person's perspective. We mistakenly think that if we acknowledge the fear or concern we are condoning it. It's better to verbalize to the other person that you are attempting to make sense of his or her perspective from the inside out. "If I felt the way you do, I'd be frustrated and hurt as well." "I don't blame you for not wanting anything to do with Christians, whom you view as hypocritical and intolerant. I'd respond the same way." Listening involves putting ourselves into the perspective of another and understanding how it feels to hold those beliefs before we evaluate or offer a retort.

Mindfulness. Mindfulness, or what activist Anna Deavere Smith calls "wide awakeness," is being fully present in the moment while engaging another person. "Mindfulness is a choice," writes Julia Wood. "It is not a talent that some people have and others don't. No amount of skill will make you a good listener if you don't make a commitment to attend to another person fully and without diversion."[20] But in our techno-driven culture of instant replies and ubiquitous electronic diversions, cultivating mindfulness is becoming a lost skill. To be mindful we need to eliminate external distractions such as vibrating cell phones or peeking at the headlines on the television screen behind the person speaking to us. As much as possible we need to create an environment where diversions are kept at a minimum. We also need to silence inner diversions such as the desire to prejudge others as soon as they bring up an issue or dismiss thoughts without fully attending to them.

The benefits of mindfulness are not restricted to communication. Mindfulness has become the focus of the United States Marine Corps. At the military base in Quantico, Virginia, soldiers receive training in mindfulness that helps them be fully present when dealing with stressful and often deadly circumstances. Psychologists who administer the training note that participants report relief from anxiety, better sleep and even improved athletic performance.[21] The most important result has been the soldiers' ability to stay calm and focused during challenging situations. Merely practicing mindfulness for five minutes a day can boost the ability to concentrate and push out distractions. The ability to stay calm and focused are the very things we need to stay committed to listening even when encountering emotionally charged language or claims we view as wrong or hurtful.

Detection of the poetic moment. In her work on listening and performance, Anna Deavere Smith believes that every person, if given enough time, will produce a moment when his or her passions surface. This moment will not only resemble poetry but also offer a deep glimpse into the person's soul. The difficulty is that in conversation, the person we are engaging will not announce that such a moment is coming or even realize that it has happened. It is up to us to recognize it, to listen look for a phrase or two that clearly lays out the person's deepest and most heartfelt conviction.

While doing graduate work I frequently collaborated with a student who was brilliant but simply couldn't meet deadlines. Our work together often resulted in tension and conflict. When it finally came to a boiling point, we sat down to discuss it. I asked him to describe his view of timeliness and deadlines, and he offered a passing remark that stood out to me—he told me that his father once called him "dumb." He had never recovered. Since that moment he had questioned whether his work, however brilliant to others, was good enough. In that one phrase I not only understood this student's struggle with meeting deadlines but also witnessed his pain. Not all poetic moments may be that clear, but we can keep listening until we feel we understand the seminal moment of a person's position. A key goal of the next step of our strategy will be to understand the factors that created that poetic moment.

STARTING A CONVERSATION WITH MARK

When I met with Mark, the graduate student abandoning his faith whom I referred to at the start of section two, I began by asking the question we've been considering: What did he actually believe? His parents had filled me in on what he was thinking, but I needed to let Mark speak for himself. After listening to him complain about the rigors of graduate school and the endless papers we had to write, I said, "Your parents tell me you're having second thoughts about Christianity. Are you?"

For the next hour Mark told me he no longer believed the narratives in the Bible were true or historical. Rather, they were carefully crafted propaganda stories told by individuals wanting to gain power or popularity. In reality, Jesus was a simple social worker who traveled the countryside helping the poor, not performing miracles or claiming to be God. The man, Jesus, was transformed into a god after his death to give his disciples credibility. As I listened I had to fight against the desire to evaluate and attempt to refute what he was saying. Only through much prayer was I able to continue to ask questions and focus on understanding.

After summarizing his thoughts, I asked what the most convincing argument was that had swayed him. "Well, my dissertation director has written extensively on this topic and his arguments make a lot of sense," Mark said. "I'm not sure there's just one argument I could identify." After taking a sip of coffee, he added, "The entire religious studies department is in agreement about what I'm saying."

In that statement I felt I had encountered a poetic moment. When Mark referred to "the entire religious studies department," I could sense his relief in finally being accepted by his peers. Having heard his reasons for moving away from conservative Christianity, I decided not to debate but move on to question two: Why did he believe these things to be true?

CONCLUSION

Communication researcher John Nyquist studied doctor-patient interactions and discovered that, on average, a patient had eighteen seconds to describe his or her problem before the doctor interrupted and started to formulate a solution.[22] How long do people have to share their perspectives with us before we jump in and take over? How much value do we place on listening, perspective taking and understanding? In surveying human behavior, the Scriptures state, "Good understanding wins favor" (Prov 13:15). Our work to attend to the perspective of others will not only help us understand them better, but also put us in good standing.

However, our attempt to listen to others is not limited to understanding what a person believes but why they believe it. The second step of our strategy attempts to discover the complex reasons why people hold the convictions discovered in step one.

SUMMARY

When trying to understand what a person believes, keep the following in mind:

Obstacles

What keeps me from understanding the viewpoint of others?

Overassessment of skills. Do I have an unrealistic view of my strengths as a listener? How would others rate my listening skills?

Prejudgment. When entering a conversation, do I think I already know what the other person will say? Am I ready to listen again to a perspective I've heard before?

Quickness to react. What emotionally loaded words set me off? Am I even-tempered or cool of spirit when discussing difficult issues?

Ambushing. Do I listen to understand or do I gather information to use against the speaker? Do people feel safe sharing information with me?

Conversational narcissism. Am I preoccupied with my own preferences, opinion or sense of self?

Message complexity. How often do I merely power browse the opinions of others rather than delving deeply into their thoughts and opinions?

Listening to Understand

In listening to understand, remember these key elements:

Desire to understand. Do we really desire to engage and understand the other person, allowing time and space to share his or her perspective?

Questions. If a phrase, term or idea is not clear, are we asking for clarification? When listening, how often do we achieve listening fidelity?

Summary statements. After asking for clarification, are we offering summary statements that paraphrase the words of the speaker, making sure to match content and tone?

Perspective taking. Are we putting ourselves into the perspective of another person to see how we would react if we held the views of the speaker?

Mindfulness. Are we fully present when listening to others? What internal or external distractions make us lose focus?

Poetic moment. Are we keeping our ears open for a phrase that surfaces a person's passion or deep conviction?

Question Two

Why Does This Person
Hold This Belief?

The Associated Press headline read, "British doctors perform heart transplant against wishes of girl."[1] The article told of a fifteen-year-old girl in northeastern England who had suffered severe heart failure and was close to death, yet refused a lifesaving operation. Parents, doctors and the local magistrate were exasperated by her unwavering refusal to agree to a heart transplant. "I don't want to die," she explained, "but I would rather die than have the transplant and have someone else's heart." The article abruptly ended with the court's decision to ignore her protests and order the operation. What was missing from this article—and what goes missing from much of our communication with those with whom we disagree— was the crucial question of "Why?" Why was a young woman with all of her life in front of her choosing certain death?

In the last chapter we examined the goal of the first step of our strategy: to determine what a person believes. In this case, the young girl believed that accepting another person's heart was wrong. The mistake her parents and the magistrate made was to neglect her perspective and hastily move on to persuasion. They encountered a viewpoint that was unacceptable and put all their time and energy into persuading the girl that her conclusion was wrong. It's easy to do, isn't it? When a person we care about holds a viewpoint we can't accept, we often respond defensively rather than pursuing further conversation. Your husband thinks sending your son or daughter to a private Christian school is being overprotective. In-laws make it known that how you are parenting is producing out-of-control children. A coworker tells you that Christians are judgmental and no one has the right to judge another person. In each case, the message is clear: You are wrong; case closed. Often we respond by defending ourselves, and tensions escalate.

Having served as mediators in thousands of difficult cases, the scholars at the Harvard Negotiation Project argue that when discussing differences, people tend to trade only conclusions, not how the different parties arrived at their conclusions. In the heat of the moment, we give the other person the bottom line of our convictions, not the backstory of how those convictions developed. The Proverbs state that "there is a way that appears right, but in the end it leads to death" (Prov 16:25). During our conversations we need to resist the urge to explain why we think the other person's position will lead to death. Rather, we need to first understand why this way seems right to him or her.

Psychologist and gender scholar Carol Gilligan states, "You cannot take a life out of history."[2] What a person believes is deeply entwined with his or her personal and social history. The second step of our strategy is to ask, "Why does this person hold this belief?" The goal is to understand why a person has embraced convictions or behaviors that we find unreasonable or offensive. The purpose of question two is to help us draw out the reasons why a person has constructed her world in a particular way.

SHAPING REALITY

While it would be impossible to list all the factors that influence a person's perspective, there are some common elements that shape how and why we interpret the world as we do.

Significant individuals. All of us have encountered individuals who have greatly influenced our thinking about ourselves and others. Social scientists refer to these people—the ones who leave the strongest imprint on us—as "significant others." These are individuals such as family, friends, coworkers, spouses, clergy and so on whose opinions matter to us and to whose messages we attach great significance. Interestingly, the people who shape our perspective are not always the people to whom we feel closest. In one study, individuals said they were more hurt by the opinions of an acquaintance they had recently met than those of a person who knew them more intimately or with whom they had a longer relational history.[3] Understanding who the significant others are in a person's life often yields important insight into how he or she has personally constructed his world.

Søren Kierkegaard is considered one of the most profound Christian writers to explore our desire for and alienation from God. In his compilation of the Danish philosopher's works, Charles Moore writes that the reader cannot understand Kierkegaard's thought without first considering four key relationships that shaped his life—an estranged father, an abandoned fiancée, a hostile editor and a beloved bishop.

Considering just two of these relationships helps us understand Kierkegaard's fascination with the theme of alienation. His father, deeply religious and melancholy, struggled to bond with his six children and established rigid rules in the home. Though distant from his father, Kierkegaard admired his piety until his father confessed to a past act of sexual impropriety. Kierkegaard's world was shattered. He would later write that his father's admission "was a great earthquake, a terrible upheaval that suddenly forced on me a new and infallible interpretation of all phenomena."[4] This revelation powerfully shaped Kierkegaard's view of relationships and his willingness to trust from that moment forward.

A fascination with alienation deepened when he made the decision to break off an engagement with his sixteen-year-old fiancée, Regine Olson. To protect her honor, Kierkegaard made the bizarre choice to purposefully and publically sully his own reputation by playing the role of a callous philanderer in hopes that people would have sympathy on her. His seemingly ill-mannered actions soon turned everyone—except Regine—against him. Her honor was protected, but he was now alone. Feelings of isolation fueled his writing and he produced a staggering thirty-five books in the next ten years.

Moore's observation that key relationships provide a context for understanding a person applies universally. With every person we encounter we could ask this question: "What relationships have influenced your life the most?" When trying to learn the history of a person's conviction, I find it helpful to ask the person to list two or three people who have influenced his or her thinking, regardless of whether this person has actually met them. Often people will list favorite authors, artists or even characters from a movie. I once had a couple tell me that the music of Bruce Springsteen had made a lasting impact on their marriage. The list yields fascinating information. Are parents mentioned, either both or one? Is a spouse conspicuously left off the list? Are any religious people referred to? If so, what faith tradition do they represent? If pressed, who would be the most influential person?

FAMILY OF ORIGIN

For many people, family members are significant influencers. The family we have grown up in has had a profound impact on the convictions, beliefs and opinions we hold now. Family relationships are considered to be the earliest and most enduring influences in how we view ourselves and the world around us. One way parents or siblings wield influence is by describing or modeling a set of rules that govern behavior within the family. One powerful set of rules is called "constitutive rules" because they define what counts within a family and how second-order realities are created. Every family has constitutive rules for what counts as respect (looking an adult in the eyes when speaking), disrespect (texting while an adult is talking), family time (television off and family playing a board game), masculinity (playing sports, doing outside chores), femininity (taking ballet, helping with cooking and cleaning) and so on. Understanding why a person holds a certain belief or conviction is often a matter of discerning a person's constitutive rules. "People have different meanings for what counts as what," notes gender scholar Julia Wood, "and we cannot safely assume that our meanings match those of others."[5]

In trying to understand why a person holds a belief it's wise to dig into his or her constitutive rules. We can ask the person to explain what in her family of origin counts as respect, love, justice, fairness, spirituality, conflict or showing interest. Then we can ask if or how she has deviated from what she learned growing up. Misunderstandings in communication often are the result of growing up in different families that have produced conflicting constitutive rules.

EXPERIENCES

Past experiences, both positive and negative, have a powerful way of shaping our expectations for the future. If you go to a restaurant and notice unsanitary conditions in the eating areas and bathrooms, that experience may prime you to notice similar conditions the next time you go out to eat. Psychologists explain that the phenomenon of priming "describes the effects of a prior context on the interpretation of new information."[6]

Growing up in east Detroit, I remember watching my parents have regular disagreements with my grandparents concerning perceived wastefulness. My grandparents, who experienced the lean years of the Great Depression, regularly thought my parents were being wasteful in what they threw away or extravagant in how they spent money. During one weekend visit, I sat and listened to my grandparents describe what life during the Depression was like. Absolutely nothing was thrown away—socks were darned, knee patches put on jeans to cover gaping holes, leftover scraps of food saved and eventually turned into a mystery casserole. For three years not a single Christmas present was purchased; rather, each present was handmade from scrap pieces of wood. Having gone though such difficult experiences, my grandparents were primed to see waste everywhere, resulting in conflict with my parents.

Often priming happens without our even being aware of it. In one study subjects were primed for hostility by watching video clips of volatile individuals such as rock star Alice Cooper and Indiana basketball coach Bobby Knight. In a second, unrelated context, these same participants were asked to listen to a speaker and describe his style. The participants perceived the speaker as hostile and competitive even though the speaker had been instructed beforehand to be noncombative. In our conversations with others, it is helpful to understand the experiences that have molded a person's perspective. Consider asking, "When did you first start to think this way?" "What experiences have shaped your thinking?" "Looking back, is there an event that crystallized your conviction?"

PERSONAL PERCEPTION

Our personal perception significantly shapes and often skews how we view others and ourselves. An attribution is our explanation of why a person acts in a certain way. A spouse doesn't help around the house because he's lazy. My boss is upset this morning because she's disappointed in me. The kids aren't excited about going to church because they're not interested in God. The explanations we use to make sense of another's actions can deeply affect our relationship with them. These explanations can also be wrong. Researchers have identified an error so common they label it the "fundamental attribution error."

This common error occurs when we overestimate the internal causes of a person's unpleasant behavior (lack of character, self-centeredness, laziness) and underestimate the external causes (not feeling well, hectic schedule, financial worries, past hurts). The opposite occurs when explaining our own undesirable behavior. To defend ourselves we overestimate external causes (the kids are distracting me, my business partner didn't do his part, I wasn't given enough time to do the project) and underestimate internal causes (I'm undisciplined, overly sensitive, unfocused).

Two communication researchers, Daniel Wann and Michael Schrader, designed an experiment to explore how this common error influences how we describe sporting events.[7] Participants watched their favorite team and were asked to explain why their team won or lost. When a team won, participants described internal factors such as dedication, teamwork and coaching. However, when the team lost, their fans consistently cited external factors that absolved the players from blame, such as biased referees, unfavorable schedule, weather or injuries.

When listening to why a person holds a particular view, we need to be aware of this common error in judgment. A friend of mine told me that his daughter once shocked him by stating that she no longer thought abortion was wrong. He became defensive and immediately assumed she was rebelling against God and the values of the family (internal factors). After a heated confrontation, he learned that his daughter's friend was pregnant and would possibly have to drop out of school. She was crushed and thought a quick abortion would remedy her friend's situation. While her moral beliefs hadn't really changed, she was overwhelmed by the plight of her friend and a host of external factors. In other words, a powerful experience and significant other was shaping her perspective. Learning this helped the father form a clearer and more complex picture of what was going on. Forming a complex view of a person requires us to consider external causes that may prompt a certain behavior or are the source of a newly formed personal conviction.

The power of individuals, family, experiences and perception to shape a person's life was on full display with the death of Steve Jobs. While Jobs is considered one our finest American inventors, his perfectionism and bouts of anger made him nearly impossible to work with, resulting in his once being fired by the very company he created. Understanding what fueled his anger and standards would have been crucial in attempting to engage him. Biographer Jeff Goodall, after being given unprecedented access to Jobs in the last years of his life, offers this insight:

> The central trauma of his life, after all, was being given up for adoption by his parents, and now he was being kicked out of his second family, the company he founded. A close friend once speculated to me that Steve's drive came from a deep desire to prove that his parents were wrong to give him up. A desire, in short, to be loved—or, more precisely, a desire to prove that he was somebody worth loving.[8]

What impact does it have on us to know that what undergirded Jobs's perfectionism and anger, at least in part, was not narcissism but the desire of an adopted kid to prove to himself and others he was worthy of love? How much would this insight change how you interacted with him?

GOALS OF STEP TWO: COGNITIVE COMPLEXITY AND EMPATHY

The goal of this second step—understanding why a person believes what he or she believes—is that by considering the many factors that shape perspective, we can form a cognitively complex view of the individual we are trying to engage. While we often have a complex understanding of those like us, we often hold more simplistic understandings of those who are different. For example, we may have an elaborate view of family members or people who go to our particular church, but we know very little about members of different denominations and even less of people from other faith traditions. The more complex our view is of another, the more sensitive we are of the influences, circumstances and motivations attached to his or her perspective. Cognitive complexity is made up of three dimensions: differentiation, abstraction and organization.

Differentiation is measured by how many distinct interpretations we have of a person's actions. If we have only one interpretation or explanation for a person's actions then we'll most likely be equally rigid in our response. Let's say you've spent hours preparing a family meal and your spouse comes home late. If the only interpretation you have is that he cares more about work than family, your hurt and anger will result in a confrontation. But what other reasons could there be for his tardiness? Was he caught in traffic? Was there a crisis at work? Did a demanding boss require he stay late? Did he have car trouble? Unfortunately, usually when we confront a person with whom we are angry, we assume we possess all relevant facts and our interpretation is unwavering.

Abstraction centers on the extent to which we interpret others' internal motives. This dimension seeks to move past surface-level observations (this person is angry, shy, prideful) to discover why a person is acting a certain way. In the case of your spouse's lateness, abstraction would force you to uncover the psychological or emotional reasons that prompt behavior. Is my spouse trying to impress his boss by putting in extra hours to compensate for a sense of inadequacy? Is he in no hurry to come home because he feels unappreciated?

The last dimension, organization, is perhaps the most important aspect of cognitive complexity. Simply put, organization is our ability to notice and make sense of contradictory information. Few people are all good or all bad. Most individuals are full of contradictions and inconsistent behavior. In his book *One Generation After*, Nobel Prize recipient and holocaust survivor Elie Wiesel attends the trial of the infamous Nazi Adolf Eichmann. He goes in expecting to see the incarnation of evil—a man devoid of goodness. But listening to others describe Eichmann Wiesel comes to a startling conclusion: "Adolf Eichmann was an ordinary man. He slept well, he ate well. He was an exemplary father, a considerate husband. . . . He was a man like any other."[9] While maintaining that Eichmann is guilty of gross atrocities, Wiesel is able to notice information that contradicts his belief that Eichmann is inhuman or demonic. Cognitively complex communicators realize that people cannot be neatly judged with broad strokes—spouses are not completely wrong, teenagers are not always clueless, and bosses are sometimes surprisingly compassionate. The ability to notice information that challenges our interpretation of others is crucial to forming complex views of those who differ from us.

I often challenge my students to form a cognitively complex view of individuals whose actions they find objectionable. In one class students are introduced to characters from the film *House of Sand and Fog*. In this movie Massoud Amir Behrani, played by Ben Kingsley, is an Iranian immigrant with shrewd business skills. When a foreclosed house comes on the market, he quickly buys it with the intention of flipping it for a significant profit. Unfortunately, the house has been wrongly repossessed by the county, leaving Kathy (Jennifer Connelly) homeless as she tries to recover from a broken marriage and alcoholism. She's emotionally unstable and desperate. When Behrani is made aware of the mistake and Kathy's misfortune he is unmoved. If she wants the house, she can buy it for the full asking price!

At this point I stop the film and ask students to form an opinion of Behrani. Most are incensed. He's a greedy businessman who is valuing a quick sale over the emotional health of a victimized, hurting woman. Based on how he's dressed and the car he drives, he obviously doesn't need the money. A few students even admit that being Iranian fuels their suspicion and anger. I then ask them to respond to the question that is the subject of this chapter—"Why does this person hold this belief?" Why does Behrani believe it's permissible to place profit over the plight of a struggling woman? When asked to form a cognitively complex view of this seemingly sordid character they object. "What is there to understand? What he's doing is wrong. Period."

If we are honest, we often adopt the same response as my students when encountering a person with whom we strongly disagree. We don't care what his or her motivations are; we're going to set this person straight. I encourage my students to work through each of the dimensions of cognitive complexity, starting with differentiation. How many interpretations of Behrani can we foster? After a long pause, the students offer alternate interpretations. Perhaps Kathy has wronged him and this is Behrani's personal vendetta. Maybe his marriage is in crisis and he's trying to placate his wife by making quick money. He has gambling debts and is trying to stave off a loan shark who is threatening his family. His son is sick and he needs quick cash for an emergency operation.

When the movie resumes we learn that the once-prosperous Behrani was a colonel in the Shah's regime but was forced to flee with his wife, adolescent son and a meager amount of money—a secret known only to him. In the States they live in an opulent apartment made possible by his secretly working as a construction worker by day and a gas attendant by night. Each night he comes home exhausted and increasingly desperate. He keeps track of every diminishing penny and knows soon he will have to tell his wife that they are broke and his son that college is out of the question. A plan begins to form when he sees an ad for a foreclosed house. If he can flip it, his secret will be safe, his marriage will survive, and his son will have his education. Driven by the Iranian value of *aberu* (saving face), Behrani conceives of and carries out a plan that must succeed. While Behrani's history does not absolve him of his callous reaction to Kathy, knowing it puts his actions in perspective and perhaps fosters empathy.

CULTIVATING EMPATHY

Emotions are a powerful indicator of how we view the world. The more forceful a negative emotion is, the more strongly we believe that something isn't right or that an injustice has been committed. If emotions are ignored, resolving differences with a person becomes increasingly unlikely. In light of this, scholars regard empathy as the "pinnacle of listening."[10] The word "empathy" comes from two Greek words that mean "in" and "feeling" and refers to one's ability to project into a person's point of view in an attempt to experience that person's thoughts, feelings and perspective. The writer of Hebrews issues a call to empathy in encouraging us to identify with persecuted Christians. We are called not only to "remember those in prison" but to do so "as if you yourselves were suffering" (Heb 13:3). We are directed to imagine being mistreated—and all the emotions associated with it—through the perspective of those imprisoned. It is one thing to understand why a person believes something; it is very different to feel the emotions associated with that belief. While empathy may be the pinnacle of listening, it is slowly becoming a lost skill.

Researchers from the University of Michigan at Ann Arbor report that since 1980 college students have shown evidence of a dramatic decline in their ability to empathize, with the steepest drop occurring in the last ten years. Utilizing the Interpersonal Reactivity Index, a questionnaire that asks individuals to respond to empathetic statements, researchers rate participants seventy-five percent less empathetic than students thirty years ago.[11] Why such a decline? While many factors are at play, some researchers suggest our lack of empathy, oddly, may be related to our reading habits. Psychologist Raymond Mar, from York University in Toronto, notes that adults who read less fiction report being less empathetic. Is it possible that fiction encourages us to understand and identify with diverse characters and the emotions they exhibit?

Empathy is fostered when we enter into another person's perspective—real or fictional—and ask, "What if?" What if I were in the situation Massoud Behrani faced in *House of Sand and Fog*?[12] How would I feel knowing that financial ruin and personal dishonor were imminent unless I flipped a house and brought in a profit? What if success were in sight only to be challenged by a woman and her lawyer? Would I be sympathetic to her situation? Would I sacrifice the needs of my family for her? Questions such as these are not limited to characters in movies or novels but can be applied to individuals with whom we disagree and find ourselves embroiled in conflict.

When seeking to foster empathy we must be careful not to question the validity of a person's emotions, even if they seem irrational or misguided. Taking a person's feelings seriously or trying to acknowledge powerful emotions is not the same as condoning the perspective that produced the emotions. Empathy communicates to another person that his or her feelings, beliefs and perspective matter and we are working to understand them.

CONTINUING MY CONVERSATION WITH MARK

How does question two relate to my interaction with Mark, the religious studies grad student brought up in a Christian home who no longer trusted the Bible?

"I don't mean to offend you," he said during lunch, "but that book has zero credibility."

The first forty-five minutes of our conversation had been spent with me inquiring about what Mark believed (question one). I now transitioned to asking why he believed what he believed (question two). How complex was my picture of Mark? How many interpretations did I have of his decision to push Christianity away? If I had only one—that he was rebelling against his parents—then my view of him was thin, not thick.

What experiences or individuals had shaped Mark's thinking? What significant others did he have in his life—individuals whose opinions mattered to him and to whose opinions he attached great significance? In learning what Mark believed I had discovered that his dissertation director, a man well-known in liberal circles as a religious authority, taught that the stories of the Bible were clever fabrications. I began to inquire about Mark's relationship with this significant individual.

Mark told me that his first meeting with this professor didn't go well once the professor learned of Mark's conservative faith. Mark desperately wanted this man to be his mentor and felt hurt by his initial rejection. In order to win over his approval, Mark agreed to be part of a study group that read articles that often challenged the authenticity of the Scriptures. His mentor asked him only to be open to the views of the group. At first Mark voiced his skepticism of what they were reading—and quickly felt the sting of disapproval. It was obvious that they thought his views were hopelessly conservative and outdated. Over time he was won over. Now I was the one with outdated views.

While it would be unfair to dismiss Mark's objections to the Bible merely as a desire to fit in, being a part of that group had greatly influenced him. As I listened it was easy to feel empathy. As a conservative Christian in higher education, I've often felt out of place in what I believe. To feel like an outsider is lonely and discouraging. Over time it can take a toll on your self-esteem. I understand the desire to be accepted and validated. These feelings of empathy helped me resist the urge to attack Mark's current views.

CONCLUSION

The purpose of asking, "Why does this person hold this belief?" is not only to trace a person's belief to its roots by understanding influential factors such as significant others, experiences and family, but also to surface and acknowledge the powerful emotions associated with these influencers. Not only will this question yield valuable information about the person we are trying to engage, it may also dramatically change the communication climate. Henry Wadsworth Longfellow writes, "If we could read the secret history of our enemies, we should find in each person's life sorrow and suffering enough to disarm all hostility."[13]

After exploring why a person holds a particular viewpoint, it's crucial to consider a question we often ignore when engaging those who disagree with us. Is it possible to discover common ground with a person who seems entrenched in an opposing view? In the next chapter we will consider the question "Where do we agree?"

SUMMARY

When trying to discover why a person holds to a particular position, try asking these questions:

Influential people

"What relationships have influenced your life most?"

"What authors or books have shaped your thinking?"

"Is there anyone who, surprisingly, didn't make your influencer list?"

"If pressed, what individual would you say has had the most impact on you?"

"Do any religious people come to mind?"

Family of origin

"In your family of origin, what counts as showing respect, love, justice, fairness, spirituality, conflict or interest?"

"How have you deviated from what you learned growing up?"

"Is there a family member or relative who significantly impacts your thinking on this issue?"

Experiences

"When did you first start to think this way?"

"What past experiences have shaped your thinking?"

"Are there experiences currently influencing how you think?"

"Is there an event or experience that has crystallized your conviction?"

Goals of step two

Keep in mind the goal of step two, first regarding cognitive complexity:

Differentiation. Am I locked into one interpretation of a person's actions, or do I have multiple interpretations?

Abstraction. Am I taking into account internal reasons why a person acts in a certain way?

Organization. Are there positive actions I'm ignoring as I form an opinion of this person?

Also consider empathy:

Am I trying to enter the perspective of a person and ask, "What if?"

How would I feel if I had his perspective?

What emotions surface as I see the situation through her eyes?

7

Question Three

Where Do We Agree?

Most of the students at the university where I teach tend to be conservative, so the controversial documentarian Michael Moore is not a household name. Many find his views hateful, ultraliberal and divisive. His documentary *Fahrenheit 9/11* is seen as a shameless attempt to use the terrorist attacks of September 11, 2001, to defame President Bush. During the documentary Moore levels more than three hundred accusations at the president, and to this day the film is the highest-grossing documentary of all time.

Frankly, my students don't care. They are offended and angry, and they want nothing to do with Moore or his movies. I'm sure it came as a surprise when those taking my advanced class in rhetoric were asked to watch and critique this documentary. Many were eager to debunk Moore. They were shocked, however, when I told them their first paper was to answer one question: Where do you agree with Moore? During the following weeks there was a steady flow to my office of students complaining they couldn't do the assignment. In the entire documentary they couldn't find one area of agreement or common ground.

How often do you and I resemble my students? When embroiled

in a heated disagreement with a person, we become entrenched in our position and completely reject the other person's arguments or accusations. I am right; you are wrong. I have no interest in considering a position I already believe to be false. Hebrew wisdom writers take a different approach when they state, "Whoever heeds life-giving correction will be at home among the wise" (Prov 15:31). Notice that the proverb doesn't say that you must agree with every rebuke but affirms the value of listening. Is any part of the rebuke true and therefore life-giving?

When it came to Moore my students focused only on the rebuke and didn't take the time to determine if there was any truth to it. I too found Moore to be offensive and often wildly inaccurate. Yet was I willing to hear him out and consider his perspective? Were there any pockets of common ground to be discovered? For example, while students may disagree with Moore's critique of then President George W. Bush, we can agree that what makes our country special is the freedom to critique a president. Having lived in the former Soviet Union for a year, I know this freedom is not to be taken lightly and is shared by liberals and conservatives alike.

In the midst of passionate disagreements differences will be apparent, and it takes skill to cultivate common ground. The third step of our strategy is to ask the oft-neglected question "Where do we agree?" In this chapter we'll take a look at the value of seeking wisdom and common ground expressed in the Scriptures, misconceptions about fostering common ground, and how to cultivate areas of agreement with those who disagree with us most.

PURSUING WISDOM

The book of Proverbs extols wisdom and encourages its readers to pursue it at all cost. Wisdom is personified as a woman calling above the roar of a busy street inviting all to come to her. The writers of Proverbs firmly believed that the voice of wisdom could be found not only in Israel but far beyond her borders as well. "All truth belonged to and ultimately derived from their Lord no matter who experienced and expressed it," writes Old Testament scholar David Hubbard.[1] This explains why the words of two non-Israelite leaders, Augur (Prov 30) and Lemuel (Prov 31), appear in the inspired book of Proverbs. They appear for the simple reason that their words reflect God's truth. The Jewish community didn't close themselves off from these leaders' perspective simply because they were outsiders. If they had, the wisdom of these men would have been lost and common ground abandoned. A key part of discernment is being willing to affirm the parts of a person's perspective that are true.

A willingness to seek common ground is on full display when the apostle Paul speaks to a diverse and potentially hostile crowd in what is commonly known as his Mars Hill discourse. Paul, in Athens, had found himself in a city saturated with idols. In fact, many Greeks at the time joked that it was easier to meet a god on the streets of Athens than a man. For Paul these idols were no laughing matter—in fact, Luke writes that when Paul saw them he was "greatly distressed" (Acts 17:16). Each idol was an affront to the holy God Paul had come to know. And yet when Paul delivers his speech at the Areopagus, he makes a fascinating rhetorical decision. "Men of Athens," he begins, "I see that in every way you are very religious" (Acts 17:22). Instead of lambasting their idols, he describes them as "your objects of worship" (Acts 17:23).

What is the Paul attempting to accomplish? First, he is carefully heeding Proverbs 18:19, which warns that an offended individual is more "unyielding than a fortified city." If he started his speech with a polemic against idols, he would risk losing them at the start. Second, Paul is choosing to focus on the struggles and questions of the Athenians, not their conclusions. He understands that each idol powerfully testifies to the Athenians' spiritual hunger. Paul is able to find common ground in their mutual questions and desires rather than become separated by differing conclusions.

In section one of this book, we examined how all reality consists of first-order realities and second-order realities. The idols Paul witnessed were first-order realities that needed explanation. What did these idols mean to his audience? The interpretation he assigned to them was that of religious yearning—a deep yearning he had also experienced prior to his conversion. Just as the Athenians had misguidedly expressed their yearning by worshiping idols, Paul had turned his yearning into persecuting the early church. This shared religious yearning, however misapplied, served as fertile common ground from which Paul could point to the "the Lord of heaven and earth" (Acts 17:24).

Paul's attempt to reach out to the audience had mixed results. Some were so entrenched in their perspective they merely "sneered" at him and left (Acts 17:32). Attempting to find common ground with others is a two-way proposition and, unfortunately, we can be rebuffed. However, others in the crowd were intrigued enough with Paul's approach and arguments that they committed to coming back to continue the conversation. A few even converted on the spot. How many would have stayed to listen if he had started his speech by saying that God, in no unqualified terms, "does not live in temples built by human hands" and that their idols were worthless (Acts 17:24)? How many more would have sneered and walked away?

Many Christians today ignore Paul's style and communicate in a way that leaves little room for common ground, as communication expert Tim Downs describes:

> A wise communicator seeks to build agreements, not arguments. *We're not that different, you and I. We come from similar backgrounds. We want a lot of the same things out of life. We only differ at this one point.* Many Christians attempt to communicate with unbelievers with a mind-set more like this: *We are completely different people, you and I. We are from different worlds. I am a citizen of the kingdom of heaven; you*

are from the domain of darkness. We think differently, we feel differently, we value different things.[2]

I can't help but wonder if so many were willing to continue the conversation with Paul outside the Areopagus because of his willingness to focus on common desires and start with areas of agreement before moving toward disagreement? Conversely, why are we so leery today of cultivating common ground with those with whom we disagree? Part of the answer is our many misconceptions of what fostering common ground means.

COMMON GROUND MISCONCEPTIONS

In today's climate of antagonistic talk radio, vitriolic political campaigns and tit-for-tat negative ads, there is simply no room for compromise or common ground. And we can't blame all our current negativity on social media or television. In 1864, while the Civil War was still being decided on bloody battlefields, George McClellan in his attempt to unseat Abraham Lincoln publically derided him as an "idiot" and "baboon."[3] When passions become inflamed, cultivating common ground is seen as a weakness. Following are the most common misconceptions that cause us to neglect focusing on where we agree with others.

Condoning. We often fear that agreeing with a person on one aspect of an issue sends the signal that we are condoning the overall message. This fear is what popular Christian author Philip Yancey encountered when he became the guest editor of *Christianity Today*. In a provocative decision, Yancey decided to explore the idea of whether Christians could learn from Mahatma Gandhi. The result was a series of articles presenting both the positive and negative aspects of Gandhi's remarkable life, along with the suggestion that Christians could learn from Gandhi's practice of spiritual disciplines, his decision to aid the outcasts of India, and an unwavering commitment to nonviolence.

While Yancey expected a negative backlash from some readers, nothing prepared him for the anger he encountered. "So, it's Gandhi on the cover this month," wrote one reader. "Who will it be next month, Ayatollah?"[4] In his articles Yancey was clear that he rejected Gandhi's decision to embrace Hinduism over Christianity, his abandonment of his wife to rescue others, and his abuse of spiritual practices that greatly hurt his health. However, was there nothing to learn from one of history's greatest activists?

When it comes to cultivating common ground, affirming part of a perspective does not mean we condone the whole. While you may strongly disagree with your boss's decision to mandate extra training that will come at great financial and personal cost, is there anything about the decision you can agree with or affirm? Or say that in her first year of college your daughter decides to stop going to church so she can check out other faith traditions. Affirming her decision to explore other worldviews does not mean you are condoning her decision to stop attending church. It's also a mistake to think that Yancey's appreciation of Gandhi's commitment to social justice meant he also affirmed Gandhi's Hinduism.

Too risky. Notice the fear undergirding the reader's response to Yancey's decision to focus on Gandhi: "Who will be on the cover next month?" If I ask the question "Where do I agree with Gandhi," what will be next? What if I find that there is so much to affirm in the views of those from different positions or worldviews that I abandon my own? If I am open to the perspectives of others, how much does this weaken my position? However, Roger Fisher and William Ury write, "It is true that a better understanding of their thinking may lead you to revise your own views about the merits of a situation. But that is not a cost of understanding their point of view, it is a benefit."[5]

One of the benefits of uncovering what's right in another person's position is that it helps uncover errors in our own. Yet we are often closed to facts that challenge us. When disagreeing with a person it's easy to stay entrenched in our position and avoid pockets of common ground that can be unsettling. It's easy to dismiss Gandhi, Michael Moore or our boss by ignoring their arguments. We call this approach "defensive listening," in which we immediately dismiss or ignore information that threatens our position. We'd rather be secure and right than open ourselves to points of agreement that might lead to a reconsideration of cherished beliefs. The third step of our strategy is often neglected because it is too risky.

An end in itself. If we are honest, many of us hate confrontation. Far from being leery of step three, we embrace it because agreeing is so much more comfortable than disagreeing. Over time we become experts at finding areas of agreement or common ground while skillfully avoiding areas of contention. As Christians who are often labeled arrogant, judgmental and intolerant, we find that it feels good to surprise people and focus on similarities. Once those areas of agreement are cultivated we are hesitant to jeopardize the positive climate by challenging others.

This is not the type of common ground advocated in this third step. Christian author and professor Daniel Taylor rightly notes that common ground "is not the flaccid 'everybody is right' of flabby relativism. The goal is not niceness, or pseudo-unanimity."[6] While cultivating areas of agreement is crucial to our overall strategy, it cannot be an end in itself. As we shall see, common ground is the place from which we seek to address areas of disagreement.

A tactic for winning. Some view creating agreement and cultivating common ground as merely a tactic to lower the defenses of others. Past experience tells us that if we go into a conversation and disagree with everything a person says, we'll make him or her defensive. Rather, we'll offer token areas of agreement so the other person will feel understood and even obligated to listen to our views. This approach to cultivating common ground is an elaborate form of ambushing where apparent lines of agreement are created simply to lure a person into a trap.

Rather than being a tactic or an end it itself, common ground is "a core package of values and rights we can affirm together while we continue to disagree on some fundamental understandings of the ultimate nature of things."[7] While our differences often hinder or even terminate communication, focusing on areas of common ground allows the conversation to continue as resolution is sought. But cultivating a core package of values, rights and areas of common ground requires skill.

CULTIVATING COMMON GROUND

The first step in fostering areas of agreement is to change our perspective as we engage others. The following suggestions may be helpful.

Look for what's right, not merely for what's wrong. Shifting our attention from noticing what's wrong with a person's perspective to what's right may not be as easy as we think. English professor Peter Elbow teaches students how to critically consider diverse viewpoints found in literature and everyday interactions. In our education, most of us have been taught what he calls "the doubting game," in which we approach others by first looking for what's wrong. Much like the press corps following the president hoping to catch him in a contradiction or playing loose with facts, we have been taught to scrutinize a perspective by doubting it. As Elbow notes, "You must assume it is untrue if you want to find its weakness."[8]

With such a mentality the first step in listening to an argument is to assume a skeptical position and try to poke holes in our opponent's perspective. As committed Christians we have become particularly adept at the doubting game. When we encounter a postmodern or atheistic thinker, our first reaction is to look for the inconsistencies or contradictions in his or her position. We'll barely tolerate Christians reading other religions' sacred writings such as the Quran or Bhagavad Gita so long as they read it to find what's wrong with it. To discover areas of agreement with those who reject our beliefs is seen as compromise.

To counter this ridged perspective Elbow advocates "the believing game," in which listeners try to "find not errors but truths."[9] The first rule of this game is to refrain from quickly judging the strange or unpleasant views of others. "This does not mean accepting everything anyone says or writes in an unthinking way," he writes. "That would be just as superficial as rejecting everything without thinking deeply about it."[10] Rather, he urges us to first give the perspective a whirl and understand the reasons why a person holds a particular view. Why does this person believe? Are there any facts, concerns or values with which we can agree? "Then you can go back and ask whether you want to accept or reject elements in the argument or the whole argument," Elbow concludes.[11]

But what should I do if I honestly cannot find any areas of agreement with my spouse or coworker? Even if I understand the value in the believing game, what if after considering the other point of view I simply don't agree with anything?

Focus on questions, not answers. The most helpful suggestion for fostering agreement when there appears to be none comes from C. S. Lewis's insightful comment about friendship. "The man who agrees with us that some question, little regarded by others, is of great importance can be our friend," Lewis writes. "He need not agree with us about some answer."[12] What often causes division is that our answers contradict each other. What may be helpful is to step away from competing answers and instead focus on the question.

I have a friend who is a committed Buddhist, and our friendship works because we value many of the same questions. In today's hurried world how can we create a sense of spirituality? What role does meditation play in fostering mindfulness? How can I incorporate my spirituality into my career? How do our actions impact others and ourselves? How should we respond when faced with suffering? In a culture where salaries, status and possessions mark a person, it's nice to have a friend who questions the status quo and is interested in pursuing spirituality. Her whole system of thought is rooted in a man who excelled in asking questions. "If you took a poll asking who the profoundest thinker of all time was, the man who would probably come out second, after Jesus, is Buddha," writes philosopher Peter Kreeft. "How can we not hear him out?"[13] While many of my final answers to life's questions ultimately diverge from those of my friend or the Buddha, our similar questions allow us to continue the conversation as we address our differences.

The importance of questions is not limited to religion. While you and your spouse may disagree on whether you should home school, focusing on the question of how to educate your children is of equal importance. Although you and your office mate disagree wildly over politics and candidates, you are encouraged that she is interested in asking how we should govern ourselves and live within a democracy. While you may have strong issue with Michael Moore's content and style, you can agree that asking how we should keep a president accountable is vital to our nation's health.

Find common values. When embroiled in a conflict we often lose sight of the bigger picture. All we can see are the disagreements in front of us. But we can foster common ground by stepping back and asking a broader question: what do we both value? At the marriage conferences where I speak, I often encounter couples who feel they don't see eye to eye on anything. I encourage them to focus on one thing they both obviously value—their marriage. While they may have differences, they both value their relationship enough to set aside a weekend, arrange a sitter for the kids, and pay hotel and registration fees.

Valuing the same thing is what holds together the most unlikely of friendships. Christopher Hitchens was an outspoken atheist who argued that religion is inherently toxic and eventually poisons everything. Larry Alex is an outspoken evangelical who runs a Christian think tank. Over the years the two would periodically debate one

another, and their disagreements were numerous. Yet here's how
Alex describes their relationship:

> We immediately discovered that we had much in common.
> We were descendants of martial traditions; we loved literature
> and history; we enjoyed lively discussion with people who
> didn't take opposition to a given opinion personally; and we
> both found small talk boring.[14]

They also loved to eat and take long car rides. After Hitchens was
diagnosed with cancer, they took a ride in which Hitchens surprised
Alex by asking him if he had a copy of the Gospel of John. He didn't,
but Hitchens did. In the back seat next to a huge container of
Johnny Walker whisky was a well-worn copy of the New Testament.
Alex describes the conversation as spirited, rational and civilized.
A few years later, Hitchens would succumb to cancer. By focusing
on common values—love of food, philosophy, politics, literature
and debate—a climate was created that allowed these two men to
slowly unpack profound differences.

Find common issues. Are there issues that warrant your setting
aside differences to work on? Colorado Springs, Colorado, is home
to two vastly different organizations. The *Independent* is a fiercely
liberal newspaper, while Focus on the Family is a staunchly conservative voice in today's culture wars. Their views on gay marriage,
abortion, politics and religion could not be more opposed. However,
readers of the *Independent* were shocked to learn the two entities
had formed a partnership. "No, hell has not frozen over," wrote the
editor. He explained that there "was at least one issue on which
Focus and the *Indy* can agree: We want all kids to grow up in a
loving home."[15] Foster care was the issue that allowed the two organizations to link arms for a common good.

Jim Daly, president of Focus on the Family, explained, "Of
course, we're going to have our differences philosophically; we understand that. But we're all big boys and girls, and so we can do the

good things that we can do for the community without giving up our principles on either side of the aisle."[16] Together they sponsored an event called "Fostering Celebration" where the focus was on the needs of Colorado's foster care system. This partnership led to Daly being on the cover of the *Independent* and an amazingly candid interview and discussion of significant issues facing Americans. Working on a common project allowed two diverse organizations to open a conversation about differences.

In our relationships, we can seek to find issues that unite us. What is it we both care about? Can we set aside differences long enough to focus on an event that will help the company grow or cause a family member to succeed? From these moments of connection and commonality a communication climate is given time to grow, which allows us to eventually address disagreements. It doesn't even matter if our motivation for addressing an issue differs.

When British Secretary of Education Michael Gove sought to place a King James Bible in the library of every state school, he found an unlikely supporter. Richard Dawkins, a militant atheist who once called God a bully and bloodthirsty ethnic cleanser, supported the idea. He was shocked that libraries didn't already have a copy. "What do they have, then? Harry Potter?" he asked.[17] Dawkins in no way views the Bible as inspired nor even as a moral guide. He does view it as a great work of literature that should be read in schools. Both men, with vastly different motivations and beliefs, used a project to cultivate common ground. In your relationships, what are the issues you can focus on as you try to work things out?

PREREQUISITE FOR COMMON GROUND

Cultivating common ground requires a sense of humility and open-mindedness. Not only do we need to listen to the views of others, but we must be willing to reevaluate what we believe. "The first to speak seems right, until someone comes forward and cross-examines him" (Prov 18:17). This proverb reminds us that we often become so convinced of our position that we forget there are always two sides to an issue.

The context of this verse is the town gate where individuals would come to present their disagreements to the local elders. First one would present his side of the issue with all his supporting facts. Next his neighbor would speak. When finished, each would, under the direction of the elders, be allowed to question each other. During the dialogue, facts would emerge that hadn't been considered and the two parties started to understand the other's point of view. "We are seldom near the truth of an issue until we hear all sides," scholar David Hubbard writes.[18] The elders would encourage compromise and resolution between the parties. Their encouragement would be successful only if both parties were willing to engage in perspective taking and acknowledge areas of agreement. If it became obvious that a person was not open, the elders would step in and offer their opinion or a well-timed rebuke. Their primary goal was to allow people to talk it out.[19] Being open to areas of agreement is what keeps a dialogue from devolving into a monologue.

CONTINUING MY CONVERSATION WITH MARK

After spending an hour listening to Mark describe how being in graduate school caused him to question his faith and the Bible, I was tempted to launch into my rebuttal. The objections he was raising were not new and I had my answers lined up and ready to go. However, doing so would entail skipping the key question we've been considering in this chapter. While it was obvious where we disagreed, were there any areas of agreement? That may seem like an odd question to ask when communicating with a person who is leaving the faith, but it is crucial to first establish points of agreement before moving to disagreement. Could common ground be culti- vated by focusing on his question rather than our differing answers?

"Can we trust the Bible?" is a question that followers of Christ often avoid. At the Christian university where I teach, I regularly ask students why they think the Scriptures are historically accurate. Do they believe the Bible is trustworthy merely because their parents, friends or professors have told them it is? If the Scriptures are not trustworthy and Christ didn't rise from the dead, then the apostle Paul himself suggests our faith is useless (1 Cor 15:14, 17). I agreed with Mark that asking questions was important and spoke well of his pursuit of knowledge—a key part of graduate school.[20]

"You can't accept the Bible just because your parents do, nor reject it because your mentor does," I said. "You have to form your own conclusions by asking and answering key questions. I applaud you for wrestling with this issue."

His response to my overture of common ground was telling. "You are the first Christian to be okay with my questioning of the Bible," he said. At that moment, I felt us make a positive turn in our discussion and the communication climate soften. If I had been defensive at his questioning of the Bible, he surely would have reciprocated and been defensive toward my defense of the Scriptures. The next step was to carefully craft my response to Mark based on what I had learned from our conversation.

CONCLUSION

When Christian philosophers Peter Kreeft and Ronald Tacelli train students to interact with people from different faith traditions, they present a series of questions seldom considered. Before asking how a religion lines up with our faith, they suggest we ask whether there are any parts of the religion that are true and if there is anything we can learn from it.[21] Not only will these two questions help us assess a particular religion, they will be helpful in forming common ground as we move from areas of agreement to disagreement with adherents of other faiths. The same two questions ought to guide our interaction with our spouse, neighbor and coworker.

One of the oldest axioms found in communication theory states, "The art of persuasion is to show that not much persuasion is needed." Our chances of persuading a person are greatly enhanced when we first uncover all the areas in which we agree before moving to areas of contention. We are much closer in our positions that you might think! It wouldn't take that much for us to agree! What keeps these sentiments from being mere play-acting or conversational manipulation is our attitude. Do we sincerely desire to learn from the other person? Are we more interested in maintaining our position than being right? Is self-interest blinding us to pockets of agreement? If we are open to life-giving rebukes, then we will not only have healthy relationships, we will be wise.

In our four-part communication strategy, the first three steps center on listening, understanding and finding common ground with another. Why do we spend so much time on the other person's view? When do we get to offer our perspective? The next chapter introduces a rule that not only undergirds the first three steps of our method but is deeply affirmed in the Scriptures.

SUMMARY

When seeking to foster common ground, keep the following in mind:

Common misconceptions

Common ground equals condoning. We often mistakenly think that agreeing with one aspect of a person's perspective means we are condoning the overall message.

Fostering common ground is too risky. If we agree with parts of another person's position, where will it lead? Defensive listening is a posture of rejecting all points of view or facts that threaten our beliefs.

Common ground is an end in itself. For those of us who hate confrontation, it is safer to focus only on areas of agreement while avoiding disagreement.

Common ground is a tactic for winning. This misconception involves fostering pockets of token agreement only to lower a person's defenses.

Cultivating common ground

Look for what's right, not merely for what's wrong.

Refrain from quickly discounting the views of others by focusing only on their errors.

Ask whether there are any facts, concerns or values with which you can agree.

Focus on questions, not answers: What common questions are we both asking? What areas do we both agree are important to ask questions about?

Common values

Step back and ask the broader question: What do we value that others don't?

Common issues

Can we set aside differences long enough to focus on an event or cause that will help the company grow or cause a family member to succeed?

The Rule of Reciprocation

Why Steps One Through Three Work

Moscow winters are brutal. The temperature frequently plunges below freezing and the wind seems to blow from all directions. What made our two-month stay even more difficult was the chilly reception we received from the manager of our hostel. She was an elderly Russian woman who spoke little English, governed with strict rules and had no patience for foreigners. If our group was a few minutes late for dinner the doors were locked and we were out of luck until breakfast. No exceptions. We resigned ourselves to a tense, awkward relationship. Who could have anticipated that in a few weeks everything would change? This hardened Russian woman went from staring at us from behind her desk to greeting us each morning with smiles and even occasional flowers. It didn't matter how late we were to dinner, she'd come out in a bathrobe, open the doors and make us something to eat.

What caused the turnaround? One wintry morning as we headed out to the metro we saw a Russian car stuck in the snow. A woman sat in the driver's seat as an elderly man futilely tried to push. Six of us walked over and in one collective shove the car was free. To our surprise, out from the driver's seat popped the manager of our hostel. For a second I thought she was going to yell at us. Instead, she was smiling and kept thanking us: "Spaceba Bolshoi! Spaceba Bolshoi!" From that moment on she was a different person.

Her change in demeanor was, in part, the result of what psychologists call the "rule of reciprocation," which prompts us to try to repay in kind what another person has provided for us.[1] By helping our hostess and her husband get unstuck that morning we communicated that they were important to us and worthy of our time and effort. Our efforts created appreciation and a sense of obligation. She felt the need to repay our kindness and it transformed our entire relationship. If properly understood, the rule of reciprocation can also transform your communication and relationships.

This powerful rule undergirds the entire communication strategy we have been considering so far and is the reason why steps one through three must be done in order. When teaching this strategy to others I've encountered a persistent objection: "Your entire strategy consists of four questions that must be asked in sequence. The first three focus on listening and creating common ground. When do I get to speak? The strategy is almost completed and I've yet to share my opinion!"

This common objection shows that many of us struggle with a form of conversational narcissism. We engage others with the goal of setting them straight. With such an attitude there is little need for understanding or common ground. But this approach often fails, and we find ourselves leaving conversations frustrated and angry. If the strategy I'm advocating in this book is going to work, we must understand the theory behind it and the indispensible part the rule of reciprocation plays in organizing our four questions. To do so, let's consider how this rule is rooted not only in culture and communication theory but also in the Scriptures.

THE RULE OF RECIPROCATION IN CULTURE

Cultural anthropologists argue that what links diverse human cultures together is a pervasive code of indebtedness. Archaeologist Richard Leakey states that there is no human society that does not adhere to the rule of reciprocation. In fact, Leakey argues that this feeling of indebtedness is a central characteristic of what it means to be human: "We are human because our ancestors learned to share their food and their skills in an honored network of obligation."[2] In order for society to work we need to believe that our actions toward others will not go unrewarded. Commerce, trade and being a good neighbor are all predicated on this rule. "With such clearly adaptive consequences for the culture, it is not surprising that the rule for reciprocation is so deeply implanted in us by the process of socialization we all undergo," writes Robert Cialdini.[3]

Parents, neighbors and teachers have ingrained the idea in us that no good deed should go unrewarded. If someone is kind to us, we feel the need to return kindness; if someone greets us with a smile we should respond similarly; if we are invited to a party, we should return the invitation. The phrase "much obliged" is rooted in this rule of human behavior. This sense of obligation is also evident in an old Japanese saying: "Nothing is more costly than something given for free." When someone acts kindly toward us we immediately feel pressed to return the kindness. Without our knowing it, this rule impacts how we communicate with our neighbors, family and coworkers.

HOW THE RULE OF RECIPROCATION SHAPES OUR COMMUNICATION

Communication theorists have been keenly interested recently in how the rule of reciprocation influences our daily interactions. Their conclusion is that the rule is pervasive and almost overpowering. In section one we discussed how our self-image is formed by the views of significant others. We care deeply about how they view us and we don't want to be seen as ungrateful or as someone who violates the principle of one good deed deserves another. "Because there is general distaste for those who take and make no effort to give in return, we will often go to great lengths to avoid being considered one of their number," Cialdini writes.[4]

One pivotal study sought to show not only the rule of reciprocation in action but also how it might cause us to overlook rudeness.[5] Cornell University researcher Dennis Regan devised a study in which two individuals attempted to sell raffle tickets. In one group, a person was instructed to act pleasantly toward others while fellow participants watched. At the end of the day this same person sought to sell raffle tickets to the group. Though the group had observed him being pleasant, few bought tickets. In a second group, a person was instructed to be rude and gruff toward others as the group watched. Then he also attempted to sell raffle tickets to participants—and sold twice as many as the person who was pleasant. Why? Before attempting to sell the tickets, he bought sodas for many people within the group. While participants felt put off by his rudeness, they also felt the need to repay him for his kind act. This rule is so powerful that it can even cause us to overlook the negative behavior of others if we feel they have given us something of value.

This rule even works with complete strangers. In one simple study, researcher Jenifer Kunz sent Christmas cards to complete strangers.[6] Recipients were randomly selected and received cards from a fictitious sender carrying the formal title of "Doctor." More than a third of recipients responded by sending their own card in return. Many of the respondents even included a personal greeting. Few felt the need to request information about the sender. They had received a card from a person they deemed important and now felt obligated to respond.[7]

This sense of obligation can even bring enemies together. Social scientist Irenaus Eibl-Eibesfeldt tells the story of a German soldier during World War I whose job it was to capture enemy soldiers for interrogation.[8] He would stealthily crawl through no-man's land and enter a trench to make his capture. On one mission, he crawled into an enemy trench, surprising a soldier eating dinner. Held at gunpoint, the frightened soldier noticed the German eyeing his bread. Unexpectedly, he offered his captor a piece. The act saved his life. The German was so moved by the gift that he simply left the trench and crawled back to his camp. The German soldier risked the anger of his superiors because he felt obligated by a single act of generosity offered by an enemy. Unknowingly, these two men experienced the principle of sowing and reaping found in the Scriptures.

RECIPROCATION IN THE SCRIPTURES

In writing to the churches at Galatia, the apostle Paul shares his own version of the rule of reciprocation. He exhorts believers not to grow weary in doing "good to all people" (Gal 6:10) and that in due time "a man reaps what he sows" (Gal 6:7).[9] If we regularly do good to others, we can expect that goodness to be reciprocated eventually. To illustrate his point Paul utilizes a practice familiar to his rural readers—harvesting. A farmer can expect to harvest only that which he has planted. You can't expect to harvest apples when you plant oranges. This same principle is true of human relationships. You cannot keep being sarcastic to your spouse and expect sympathy; you cannot neglect a relationship with a neighbor and expect it to thrive. What Paul is saying has great consequence to us as communicators and reflects the core truth of the rule of reciprocation. We can expect to be treated in the same manner in which we treat people. The generosity we show to others will be repaid. How can we be so sure? God himself ensures that this universal pattern is followed.

To drive home this point Paul declares, "God cannot be mocked" (Gal 6:7). Bible expositor John Stott takes note of Paul's use of the word "mock": "The Greek verb here (*mukterizo*) is striking. It is derived from the word for a nose and means literally to 'turn up the nose at' somebody and so to 'sneer at' or 'treat with contempt.'"[10] In our interactions with others we need to remember that God will not allow us to turn up our nose at his principle of sowing and reaping and still expect to have healthy relationships. We cannot be harsh toward others and expect compassion in return. We cannot dominate the conversation and then expect people to be silent when we are speaking. We cannot fake interest in others so they'll feel indebted to listen to us. For those of us attempting to heal a tense relationship this is good news. Based on this enduring principle, it's reasonable to expect that if we keep being kind and compassionate to an individual we will one day reap the benefit.

APPLYING THE RULE OF RECIPROCATION TO OUR STRATEGY

The Scriptures suggest that our personal actions operate according to a cause-and-effect pattern. When we reach out to others they generally will feel indebted to reach out to us. This pattern of interaction suggests incorporating the following steps into our strategy.

Start the conversation right. How we start a conversation is the most important decision we'll make and will determine if the discussion is productive or divisive. Communication researcher John Gottman argues that the first minute of interaction between individuals sets the tone for the entire conversation. That's why those of us who study communication call the first minutes of a conversation the "critical startup." If you start a conversation by forcing your views on the other person it will set an aggressive tone to the discussion. Conversely, if you show empathy, it will set a compassionate tone as you discuss differences. The first three steps of our strategy ask you to start the conversation by listening, seeking to understand and fostering common ground. Doing so not only sets a positive tone but acknowledges the power of the rule of reciprocation. As we move through the first three steps, individuals will gradually feel the increasing desire to repay our attentiveness. "Well, I've been doing all the talking," they might say. "What do you think?"

Work with the rule, not against it. Marketers looking to manipulate the public did not create the rule of reciprocation. Rather, our Creator instilled it in us. In advancing the idea of sowing and reaping the apostle Paul argues for a "principle of order and consistency which is written into all life, material and moral."[11] Culture itself is based on the pervasive idea that how you treat others is how you'll be treated. Theologian Cornelius Plantinga summarizes this universal pattern:

> Like yields like. You get back what you put in. What goes around comes around. . . . No matter what we sow, the law of return applies. Good or evil, love or hate, justice or tyranny, grapes or thorns, a gracious compliment or a peevish complaint—whatever we invest, we tend to get it back with interest. Lovers are loved; haters, hated. Forgivers usually get forgiven; those who live by the sword die by the sword.[12]

The first three steps of our strategy are built on Plantinga's observation that whatever we invest we get back with interest. In engaging others will we work with the rule or against it? If we want our friends and neighbors to listen to our story, then we must listen to theirs. If we want others to attend to our convictions then we must first attend to theirs. If we desire for others to cultivate common ground with us, we must do so first. In doing so we will create a communication climate in which we can fulfill one of our deepest longings—to talk productively about issues that separate us.

OBJECTIONS

When people first become aware of how the rule of reciprocation shapes communication, they have two common reactions. First, isn't utilizing the rule manipulative? Advertisers, marketers and overly aggressive recruiters regularly abuse this rule. Gifts, free samples of food and no-obligation trials are ways to engage the rule we've been discussing. I give you something; you feel compelled to give me something.

We've all had the experience of being at an impasse with a salesperson over the price of a car or appliance. A favorite sales technique is for the salesperson to say he or she will talk to the manager to see if the price can come down. When the salesperson comes back with the good news of a lowered price, the rule of reciprocation has been invoked and you feel pressure to respond. If you still waver, the salesperson is more than willing to go back again to see if the price can come down even further, knowing this will make you feel more indebted. The manager and salesperson are counting on you to feel an increasing need to reciprocate their apparent generosity.

The rule is also at play when salespeople use the large-request-then-small-request sequence. One billiard table manufacturer instructed salespeople to first show potential buyers the most expensive billiard table on the floor knowing that the majority of customers would decline such a pricey purchase. The salesperson counteroffers by showing customers a more reasonably priced model that was the goal all along. His or her concession makes you feel obligated to purchase the second model. In one store the tactic was wildly effective, resulting in shoppers making an average purchase of $1,000.[13]

Yes, the rule of reciprocation can be used to pressure or manipulate people to do what we want. If the only reason we listen or cultivate common ground is to make a person feel indebted to do the same, we are merely using the rule as a means to secure our real goal—presenting our opinion. But as Christian communicators we are commanded to honor others and put their needs above our own (Rom 12:10). We seek to understand because the person we are engaging is unique and deserves our honor and attention. What keeps the first three steps from being an elaborate sales tactic is our desire to cultivate an authentic conversation where both sides are heard. By utilizing the first three steps of our strategy we are working with the rule to create a give-and-take dialogue where each person feels compelled to return attentiveness and understanding.

The second objection focuses on our doubts about the rule itself. Think of a spouse, child or coworker who has consistently rebuffed your attempts to be gracious. In spite of your best efforts, this individual has rejected your overtures and the relationship continues to decline. You sow civility but reap only sarcasm. Paul's admonishment to not grow weary is becoming more challenging and unrealistic. What's to be done?

As we discussed earlier, it is imperative to regularly practice key spiritual disciplines as we reach out to others. I particularly find the discipline of worship to be useful in combating discouragement. The more I focus on the faithfulness of God, the more I can trust that he is using my respectful and gracious disposition to impact others. Do I trust God that he will use my actions to influence another? "If your enemy is hungry," states Paul, "feed him" (Rom 12:20). In doing so, your actions become "burning coals" of conviction used by the Spirit. If even enemies can be swayed, how much more those we care about? What often discourages me most is the lack of immediate results. I've sowed good deeds but have yet to reap anything.

Bible commentator John Brown reminds us that central to the harvest metaphor is patience. "Christians frequently act like children in reference to the harvest," he writes. "They would sow and reap in the same day."[14] But just as a farmer allows seeds to germinate and grow, we need to let our kind actions take root in a person's life and gradually grow in influence. The disciplines of worship and meditation help us to focus on the one who promises that the good we do toward others will not go unnoticed or unrewarded (1 Pet 3:12).

The power of the rule of reciprocation to strengthen relationships was on full display when then president-elect Barack Obama made a controversial decision to ask evangelical pastor Rick Warren to pray at his inauguration. The move angered many of the president-elect's supporters who fiercely opposed Warren's stance on abortion and gay marriage. While Obama also disagreed with many of Warren's views, he would not waver from his decision. What fueled his resolve? He was moved by a deep feeling of indebtedness. "I would note that, a couple of years ago, I was invited to Rick Warren's church to speak, despite his awareness that I held views that were entirely contrary to his when it came to gay and lesbian rights, when it came to issues like abortion."[15]

Two years before Obama's historic inauguration, Warren had made an equally controversial decision to invite Senator Obama to speak at his annual AIDS conference at Saddleback Community Church. While he opposed Obama's stance on abortion, Warren admired the senator's unwavering commitment to AIDS victims. Many Christians openly criticized Warren and claimed Obama's presence would revoke God's blessing and lead people astray. Warren would not be dissuaded and Obama addressed the conference. It was a decision President Obama never forgot. Moved by Warren's respect for him he repaid his debt by showing equal respect to Warren and placing him on the world's largest stage. Those feelings not only helped both men move past differences but kept communication alive.

The first three steps of our strategy are designed not only to help us understand the differences that separate us, but to create a reciprocal communication environment of understanding, acknowledgement and common ground. This environment is crucial for the last step of our strategy: discerning the best way to present our perspective.

SUMMARY

The rule of reciprocation is rooted in culture and communication.

Rule of reciprocation. We should try to repay in kind what another person has provided for us.

Rooted in culture. There is no human society that does not adhere to the rule; a feeling of indebtedness is a central characteristic of what it means to be human.

Rooted in Scripture. The apostle Paul shares his own version of the rule when he states that "a man reaps what he sows" (Gal 6:7).

Applying the rule to our communication

Start the conversation right. The first minute of an interaction sets the tone for the entire conversation.

Work with the rule, not against it. If we want others to listen to our story, we must listen to theirs. If we want others to cultivate common ground with us, we must do so first.

Common objections

Utilizing the rule is manipulative. While the rule can be used to manipulate, it also can be utilized to create an authentic give-and-take conversation where both sides feel affirmed.

The rule does not always work. In spite of our best efforts, people will reject our overtures of kindness and civility. God has promised that the rule applies in all interactions and that in due time a person will reap what he or she sows.

Question Four

Based on All I've Learned, How Should I Proceed?

In the movie *Groundhog Day,* an egotistical meteorologist named Phil (played by Bill Murray) is miserable at the thought of having to cover Groundhog Day for the fourth consecutive year in the boring town of Punxsutawney, Pennsylvania. Phil hates everything about the tradition and the people. Unexpectedly, he finds himself living the same day over and over in a bizarre time loop. Each morning he wakes at precisely six a.m. and begins a replay of the previous day. From morning to evening he encounters the same individuals and has the same conversations.

This proves helpful in his interaction with a love interest, Rita, who is initially put off by his self-absorption and sarcasm. When he learns that she studied nineteenth-century French in college, he laughs. Her hurt expression prompts him to adjust. The next day (which is the same day repeated) she tells him again of her studies, and he responds approvingly in perfect French.

"You speak French?" she asks.

"Oui," he replies.

After spending weeks in a hedonistic romp resulting in bouts of depression, Phil slowly starts to reexamine his life and relationships. Building on his knowledge of people, he begins to change how he speaks to others. Not every conversation can be about him. He comes to understand what is important to each person, why the conversation eventually breaks down, and how he needs to adjust.

How many times have you or I wished we could redo a conversation—to go back twenty-four hours and start over? What adjustments would we make? What would or wouldn't we say? Our ability to adapt how we speak to specific individuals in certain situations is considered by communication scholars to be the most complex and effective skill we can develop. The last step of our communication strategy focuses on one issue: What should we do once we have listened to a person and cultivated common ground? After completing steps one through three of our method, how should we respond?

The answer in part comes in the book of Proverbs' careful description of how a discerning person sets out to build a house of wisdom. Proverbs 24:3-4 tells us, "By wisdom a house is built, and through understanding it is established; through knowledge its rooms are filled with rare and beautiful treasures." This proverb mirrors the communication methods we have been considering. In step one, by asking, "What do they believe?" we are gathering knowledge—facts, information, beliefs and convictions. In steps two and three, the answers to "Why do they believe?" and "Where do we agree?" help us prioritize facts and cultivate common ground, which is the foundation of true understanding. Step four requires that we allow our personal communication to be molded by wisdom—in this case, the artful application of knowledge and understanding to people. In this chapter we'll consider what constitutes person-centered communication, the common mistakes we make, and how to set communication goals.

PERSON-CENTERED COMMUNICATION

When engaging others in conversation, we tend to fall into one of two orientations—we are either position-centered or person-centered. Position-centered individuals view others as a collective whole based on gender, race, education level, social position, political affiliation, religion and so on. Individuals are grouped into large, often stereotypical categories and are treated accordingly. As a professor I find it easy to assume a position-centered stance toward my students. Since I teach upper-class courses filled with seniors, I assume that all of my students are stressed about graduation, fixated on the job market, in denial about student loans and mentally checked out. I know that's how I felt when I was in college and I assume they are like me. My communication with individual students is governed by how I expect them to act as a collective whole.

We also adopt this orientation when we assume all men or husbands are this and all women or wives are that. As parents it's easy to think that kids born into this techno-savvy generation are collectively distracted and amused to death. As Christian communicators we often adopt a position-centered approach to others when we learn they are atheist, postmodern, Muslim or of a different political party. Our bookstores are filled with books about individuals who are different from us. We depend on social researchers such as George Barna to paint a picture of the statistic—be it a non-Christian or a Christian with a different theological grid. While this information is valuable as a type of introduction, key questions must be asked: Are we relating to a person or someone's analysis of them? Do we allow individuals the freedom of self-definition? Have we boxed people in according to stereotype? How much of my communication is shaped by prejudgment?

The danger with a position-centered orientation, writes Christian author Eugene Peterson, is that it turns a "person into a flat and featureless generality, identified by a label."[1] Peterson points out that a label is only marginally useful for understanding some aspect of a person. The risk of putting labels on people is that they obscure the very thing as Christians we should be interested in, "the unprecedented, unrepeatable soul addressed by God."[2]

Because each person is an "unrepeatable soul," we must adapt our communication to the person. A speaker who adopts a person-centered rather than a position-centered approach is one who "is able to anticipate how different individuals might respond to a message, and adjust his or her communication accordingly," says communication researcher Em Griffin.[3] Learning to adjust our message to a particular person is central to our maturing as an individual and communicator. George Herbert Mead, a psychologist and communication expert whose work has shaped much of our current understanding of communication, argues that central to a child's development is the ability to understand a person's frame of reference, which he calls "role-taking."[4] Much can be learned about a child by how much he or she adapts communication to the thoughts and feelings of others.

In one study, second- to ninth-grade schoolchildren engaged in a role-playing exercise in which they were asked to convince a woman to adopt a lost puppy. The messages varied greatly. Some children neglected to take into consideration they were talking with a grown-up who might have concerns that a child wouldn't. Others recognized the difference but didn't alter their message. Some children clearly showed evidence of considering objections the woman might have. For example, puppies chew furniture. The most sophisticated children anticipated this objection and specifically addressed it, saying, "While you might have to put up with a puppy for a while, he'll eventually grow into a faithful companion you'll have for years."[5]

How much does our communication mirror that of these young communicators? Do we assume most people see the world as we do? Do we consider the other person's point of view before we speak? Do we acknowledge objections? Most importantly, are we able to alter our message to match the perspective of the other person? Mediation experts Fisher and Ury argue that when we are in the midst of intense disagreements it is crucial to consider why a person has not already made the decision you are advocating. "What interests of theirs stand in the way?" they write. "If you are trying to change their minds, the starting point is to figure out where their minds are now."[6]

Central to person-centered communication are the habits of seeing the situation through the eyes of the other person, recognizing potential objections, acknowledging common ground and tailoring our message to fit the situation. Of course, many of us fail to be person-centered for many reasons. Before discussing how to respond to a person, let's consider two common mistakes we make when it's our turn to talk.

COMMON MISTAKES

In every conversation there comes a pivotal time when we have the opportunity to respond to what the other person has said. These are common mistakes we often make:

Avoiding difficult issues. The benefit of steps one through three is that by focusing on listening, understanding and cultivating areas of common ground, we help create a positive communication climate. We are encouraged that the conversation didn't immediately deteriorate into arguing. The person we're engaging feels, perhaps for the first time, valued and acknowledged. It feels good to talk without tension. Understandably, when it comes time for us to speak and share our concerns, we are hesitant to ruin the positive atmosphere. So we downplay our concerns and avoid sharing hard truths.

In a survey of 1,800 physicians nationwide, more than half admitted that they'd described someone's prognosis in a way they knew was "too rosy." When the moment came to share discouraging news, they wavered. The "untruths were given to give hope," researchers say.[7] While it is wise to first build a positive communication climate before sharing opinions we suspect will strain the conversation, it is a mistake to consistently avoid hard issues. Referring to an ancient custom in which trusted friends greeted each other with a kiss, Hebrew counselors state that an "honest answer is like a kiss on the lips" (Prov 24:26). Honesty communicates trust. If the time never seems right to address honest disagreements, then we have fallen into this common mistake.

Telling it like it is. When embroiled in disagreement, some individuals adopt the philosophy of "shooting straight" with a person. Being real or authentic is their highest value. Philosopher Gregg Ten Elshof identifies such people as being "hyper-authentic" and gives the following caution:

> If you get a compliment from a hyper-authentic person, take heart: it's nothing short of absolutely sincere. But if you've managed to offend him, well, you better take cover. "I will be absolutely true to myself and others. . . . It may be painful for those around me. But it will be true. No façade. No make-believe."[8]

For these people, it's always the right time to give an honest answer and tell the other person exactly how they assess the situation. Taking time to listen and understand is seen as beating around the bush and delaying the inevitable. Better to get all the cards on the table and then deal with the fallout. They fully take to heart the apostle Paul's instruction to speak truth to each other and are less concerned with the love component. Hyper-authentic people also fail to heed the book of Proverbs' observation that a wise communicator "finds joy in giving an apt reply—and how good is a timely word" (Prov 15:23). To think that it is always time for being brutally honest is to violate the core of person-centered communication. Deciding what and how to share our concerns will be determined by asking one key question.

CULTIVATING PERSON-CENTERED COMMUNICATION

"The heart of the righteous weighs its answers" (Prov 15:28). The word "weighs" literally can be translated "meditates" or "studies." What is it we should meditate on or study before we offer our opinion? We should consider all we've learned from engaging in steps one through three with a person. What does this person believe? Why does he or she believe this? Where do we agree? Once we've meditated on our answers, we then should ask, "With this person, at this time, under these circumstances, what is the next thing I should say?"

With this person. The first quote many of us learned in history class comes from American philosopher George Santayana: "Those who cannot remember the past are condemned to repeat it."[9] What is true for our study of history is equally true for our relationships. The most important variable in our conflict with others is our relational history with them. Our past interactions bleed into present conversations. Before speaking it is crucial that we assess our history with this person. How have we resolved conflict in the past? Did one tend to dominate another? How angry was the exchange? Did I feel attacked or acknowledged? Are there any lingering feelings or regrets? Not only do we tend to dwell on past interactions, but we carry those emotions and perceptions into the present. If our history with a person is poor then we must adapt our communication goals.

If there is a negative history it will be prudent to spend time repairing one or more of the elements of the communication climate—acknowledgement, trust, commitment and expectations. Based on your past which element needs to be addressed? For example, if in your last conversation with your spouse you both neglected to acknowledge the other and spoke with raised voices, that exchange will color your expectations heading into the next conversation. Your recollection of the past—filled with powerful emotions—now serves as the backdrop for future exchanges. To ignore that history will ensure you will repeat it. But if I know I failed to acknowledge you or keep my voice down, this helps me craft my response to you the next time we discuss this issue. My priority will be to practice mindfulness, acknowledge your position and keep calm. Person-centered communication requires that we adapt not only to the person but also to the relational history. No doubt our ability to focus on the other person and control our passion will be based on carefully practicing relevant spiritual disciplines well in advance of the conversation. We cannot merely will ourselves out of past habits or patterns of interaction.

At this time. No conversation happens in a vacuum. In the class I teach on family communication I ask students to list the challenges parents encounter while trying to raise a family. Common answers include marital struggles, demanding work schedules, financial challenges, relocating, health issues, problematic relatives and so on. All of these factors no doubt produce varying levels of stress and tension that greatly influence their parenting. It would be foolish to judge our parents without taking these factors into consideration. The same is true of the person with whom we are disagreeing. At the same time a person is trying to resolve an issue with us, he or she is also trying to manage life and all the stress that comes with it.

One of the key mistakes we make in engaging others is to neglect to take into consideration the complexity of their overall lives and whether this is a good time to address a particular issue. Before launching into a conversation we need to understand what is happening in the other person's world. What level of stress is he or she experiencing? It's important we distinguish between a stressor event and stress itself. A stressor event is an incident or circumstance—a test, in-laws visiting, a doctor's appointment, graduation, a credit card bill, a holiday, preparing taxes—anything that has the potential to cause tension or stress in a person's life. Stress is a person's perception of the stressor and his or her resources to deal with it.

For many of us a flat tire (stressor event) is merely an irritation because we have roadside service that can quickly fix it (resources). For the working poor a flat tire means that the car is out of commission because there are no resources to fix it, resulting in significant stress. Stressor events also affect our relationships. My wife knows that after years of experience I don't usually get stressed by public speaking. Even as a conference approaches she can talk to me about important issues or sensitive topics. However, if I'm speaking at an academic conference on a technical topic in front of a room full of specialists, then it's best to wait until the conference is over to discuss important topics. If she tries to address an issue when a stressor event is so close, I will be unfocused and irritable, resulting in a frustrating conversation. Person-centered communication requires that we know not only what's going on in a person's life before engaging them, but also the stress these events are producing.

Under these circumstances. Even if the relational history is positive and the level of stress manageable, it is crucial to consider whether the setting and the timing are conducive to discussion. If mindfulness is a key part of any conversation, then we need to control the environment and pick the time carefully. Are there kids clamoring for attention? Is the television blaring in the background? Are we in a public place where it's difficult to talk? Are we trying to fit a conversation in even though we need to be somewhere in a half-hour? My wife knows that the worst time to talk about issues is when we are getting ready for bed. I'm tired and just want to sleep. The best time is after dinner while drinking we're coffee. After a good meal she can tell me anything!

"Honey, half the house burnt down today."

"It happens," I respond, sipping from my cup.

What is the next thing I should say? Notice our question ends with asking what is the next *thing* we should say, not multiple *things*. Part of weighing our response is to prioritize. Entering a conversation we often desire to address many topics and finally get these issues resolved. Agenda setting is the practice of determining and prioritizing what we want to say. If there are three or four issues we want to address, we need to force ourselves to rank them according to what is best for this person at this time. Bracketing is the process of recognizing legitimate issues that come up but don't fit your agenda. Make a mental note to return to those issues when the time is right.

While all of this may sound good on paper, the greatest challenge will be what communication scholars call "agenda anxiety," which is the overall fear that we won't cover everything during one conversation. Due to our dread of conflict we often want to resolve all issues in one setting so we won't have to have this talk again. We make a mental list of all we want to share and commit ourselves to leaving nothing unsaid. Better to push through and get everything out on the table than to have to have another uncomfortable conversation. While such a fear is understandable, it undermines the question we've been considering: "With this person, at this time, under these circumstance, what is the one thing I should say?" The goal is not to resolve all issues but to construct a productive and healthy conversation, which may require leaving some subjects for a future conversation. Your ability to prioritize will be based on what your goal is for a particular discussion.

COMMUNICATION GOALS

Most of us enter a conversation without a clear goal for what we want to happen. And this lack of clarity greatly diminishes our chances of having a productive exchange. Conflict resolution experts Wilmot and Hocker suggest four goals people pursue while trying to resolve differences. Each requires a different focus and set of skills.

Topic goals: What do we want? Wilmot and Hocker note, "Topic goals can be listed, argued, supported by evidence, and broken down into pros and cons."[10] With topic goals, we need to be able to articulate exactly what we want and provide evidence for why it's the right course of action. For example, say you have a teenage son who is driving you crazy by being constantly plugged into technology. You want to set clear limits when it comes to social media, video games and texting. Specifically, you want him to stop texting during dinner and go on social media only when all homework is completed. Assenting to these restrictions is what you want from your son. Advocating for these restrictions will require you to offer an explanation and evidence of some kind as to why they are valid. No doubt your son will also have topic goals for the conversation, such as protecting his freedom and proving you wrong. While topic goals are often are apparent to participants, they are not the only or most important goals in a conversation.

Process goals: What communication process will be used? Process goals address our meta-communication—communication about our communication. As we head into a conversation, we usually have an idea of how the interaction should be structured: each of us will have equal time to talk, interruptions will be kept to a minimum, there will be no shouting, and we will work toward consensus when possible. Our process goals shift depending on whom we are engaging. While I don't expect my boss to talk to me like my spouse, I do expect that our conversation will be professional as we discuss differences.

Going back to the example of your son, a significant process goal might be to help him understand how to have a mature, respectful conversation. If there is a poor relational history between you and your son, then having a structured conversation where each person feels heard might be a more important goal than actually resolving the issue during that specific talk. Before the conversation even begins it is crucial to define what maturity, respectfulness and being heard mean to each of you and how to facilitate these attributes in your conversations.

Identity or face-saving goals: Who am I in this interaction? As the tension increases in an interaction, individuals often begin to ask, "How can I protect my self-identity during this conflict?" If you perceive you are being slighted, ignored, bullied or humiliated, the desire to save face can become your primary goal. The concept of a "face" in communication is used to describe the sense of self we carry into disagreements and how we perceive others view us either positively or negatively. "In some instances, protecting against loss of face becomes so central an issue that it swamps the importance of the tangible issues at stake and generates intense conflicts that can impede progress toward agreement and increase substantially the costs of conflict resolution," writes B. R. Brown.[11] Wilmot and Hocker concur: often, what I want from you is the "result of what I think you think about me."[12]

All of us have experienced a situation where it becomes obvious that we were wrong. We realize that our facts were incorrect or our memory faulty. In those situations we can easily become consumed with showing others that while we may have been wrong about one issue, we are still competent and correct on other issues. But in attempting to persuade others, we need to pursue a resolution that allows all parties to save face in forming a compromise. Is there a resolution both you and your son can adopt that allows you each to save face? Or are you trying to prove your son is completely wrong about the dangers of social media and is simply naive? If so, your son may adopt a goal of saving face and continue to argue so as not to be embarrassed by conceding.

Relational goals: Who are we to each other? While process goals structure a conversation, relationship goals "define how each party wants to be treated by the other and the amount of interdependence they desire."[13] Relational goals are often at the heart of a conflict and can easily derail an entire conversation. They play a significant role in communication because every message has a relational element to it. For example, while it's important to you that your son reel in his use of social media, it is imperative that he be respectful while discussing differences. A key goal for you is that the conversation will reflect how a parent and child should respectfully and lovingly treat each other, even while disagreeing. If the conversation becomes heated or antagonistic, then your goal shifts from addressing a topic—limiting social media—to a relational one of restoring civility and respect. "Relational interests carry more urgency than topic interests," conclude Wilmot and Hocker.[14]

CONTINUING MY CONVERSATION WITH MARK

After listening to Mark share why he doubted his faith and the Bible, I was trying to determine which communication goal would be appropriate. I decided to select a process goal and focus on how we could structure future conversations. It was unrealistic to think that I could talk him out of his doubts in one lunch. If we continued to meet to discuss this issue, how should we interact? Since he did most of the talking this time, should I expect to do all the talking next time? I decided to make him an offer. What if we both recommended one book to each other that represented our differing views? After we had read them, we could discuss their merits. He agreed. We decided that the next lunch would entail giving a quick synopsis of the book we'd been given and a report of how we both agreed and disagreed with the authors. He quickly recommended a book by the liberal theologian Bart Ehrman and I suggested a classic work by theologian F. F. Bruce titled *The New Testament Documents: Are They Reliable?*

Choosing a process goal allowed me to set the stage for future conversations and hopefully ensure they would be productive. As we left I was pleased in knowing that in a short time my view of Mark had grown more complex, my understanding of why he doubted his faith had deepened, and he had agreed to meet with me again. In our next lunch I'd make sure to again utilize the communication strategies we've been discussing.

CONCLUSION

As Christian communicators there is one relational goal that applies to all of us regardless of person or situation. The Scriptures specifically admonish us to be gentle in our communication. In addressing those caught in sin we are to restore them "gently" (Gal 6:1). When defending the Christian worldview we should do so with "gentleness and respect" (1 Pet 3:15). Regardless of how those who oppose us act, we are to "gently instruct" them in hope that God will grant repentance (2 Tim 2:25). Paul states that his desire when confronting disobedient members of the church at Corinth is to have "a gentle spirit" (1 Cor 4:21) rather than being heavy-handed in discipline.

The difficulty modern readers have with such commandments is that gentleness is often seen as weakness. The Greek word most associated with gentleness is "meekness." In English, "meek" comes from an Old Norse word meaning "soft." When disagreeing with others, the last thing we want is to be viewed as is soft. Soft people get pushed around and manipulated. However, gentleness and meekness are also associated with words such as "humble," "tolerant," "tenderhearted" and "unpretentious."

Few would think that the apostle Paul was soft when confronting others. He didn't think he was better than those he sought to correct but resolved to present his case in humility. When responding to others, we must adopt the relational goal of addressing another gently. Are we tenderhearted even in our deepest disagreements? Do we humbly acknowledge that our view is not always right? Are we tolerant of views that are different? A gentle approach will not only set the relational tone for future interactions but will bring affirmation of the Spirit. "To be gentle is to be blessed," concludes the ancient church father Gregory of Nyssa.[15]

Now that we've considered the four steps of our strategy, you may be wondering how it works in practice. In the next section we'll apply our strategy to three scenarios that challenge our commitment to gentle, person-centered communication. How should I respond to my spouse when it comes to disagreements over finances? Is it possible to discuss religion without offending a person? Can I discuss an unhealthy preoccupation with video games with my teenager without pushing him away?

SUMMARY

When it's your turn to respond keep these principles in mind:

Position-centered versus person-centered
Do I view people as a collective whole based on gender, race or education, or do I treat each person as an unrepeatable soul created by God?

Common mistakes
In an attempt to keep the peace do I regularly avoid difficult issues? In a difficult conversation is my highest priority to be hyper-authentic and tell the brutal truth?

An important question
As you respond, keep in mind an oft-neglected question: "With this person, at this time, under these circumstances, what is the next thing I should say?"
   Person. What is my relational history with this individual?
   Time. What stressors is a person experiencing heading into conversation?
   Circumstances. Is the time and setting conducive to a productive conversation?
   One thing. Have I prioritized and created an agenda for what I want to say?

Communication goals
Topic goals. What do we want?
   Process goals. How will conversation be structured?
   Identity or face-saving goals. Who am I in this interaction?
   Relational goals. Who are we to each other?
   Nonnegotiable goal. Regardless of the person or situation, we are all called by God to be gentle in our communication.

Putting it into Practice

Praxis *is a Greek word combining theory and practice. In section one we considered the power of words, how our emotions are fostered, what causes conflict, and the role spiritual disciplines play in helping us engage in gentle communication. Section two introduced four questions that help organize a conversation and maximize the rule of reciprocation. Each question helps move the conversation along in productive ways. The observations in these chapters are rooted in communication theory and supported by research. The time for theory is over.*

But how might these principles work in a real conversation where disagreements are obvious and emotions run high? In each of the following scenarios we'll listen in as a person familiar with our method seeks to apply it. While each case study may not exactly correspond with your particular situation or issue, it will be helpful to observe the principles of this book in action. As you place yourself in each situation, what advice would you give based on the principles we've been considering? I'll offer comments and advice as the conversation unfolds.

Case Study One

Disagreeing
About Finances

Talking about budget, spending habits, savings and debt can cause much strife for couples. Contrasting perspectives on these issues often lead one partner to think the couple is doing well with finances while the other thinks they are being irresponsible. Financial struggles are considered one of the most significant causes of divorce in America. For Christian couples, discussing what constitutes living by faith or trusting God compounds this issue. In the following scenario we follow a wife who disagrees with her husband about how to respond to a pressing need presented by the pastor of their local church. For the sake of the following scenario we'll assume Amanda is familiar with the concepts we've been considering. Her challenge is to now put these principles into practice.

SETUP

The pastor concludes his sermon by reading a well-known passage: "Without faith it is impossible to please God" (Heb 11:6). "How should we respond to this?" he asks. Amanda and Tyler, along with the rest of the congregation, sit in silence. "This morning we have a unique opportunity not only to put our faith into action, but to please God."

He explains that a missionary serving in Taiwan has made known to him a desperate need. His ministry centers on helping young girls—some as young as six and seven years of age—escape from sex trafficking. The key to helping them escape is to find safe housing once they flee their situation and captors. Unexpectedly, two buildings have become available that would be perfect for housing dozens of women. By faith the minister scratched together enough money—all he has—to make a down payment. But he'll lose the buildings and the money if he doesn't come up with the first payment within two weeks.

The pastor implores the church to consider giving generously. "The question each of us needs to ask is, will we trust God or not? He's gone all in—will we?"

During the drive home after the service there is an uncomfortable silence between Amanda and Tyler. The kids in the back ask what's for lunch, providing the only break in the silence. Without saying a word, each knows what the other is thinking. Tyler wants to respond by giving sacrificially, while Amanda is worried about over-committing. On several occasions Tyler has wanted to respond to similar needs by giving an amount that will stretch their faith and checkbook. He's expressed frustration that Amanda often acts like a speed bump to his living a life of faith. She feels that her fears and concerns are ignored and that she's seen as uncommitted.

"I would like to talk about what the pastor said," Tyler says, helping their youngest out of her car seat. Amanda immediately feels an ache in the pit in her stomach. Discussing finances has not gone well in the past and this could add fuel to an already simmering fire. Yet they have to talk.

While Amanda is familiar with the concepts we've been considering in this book, how does it look to put them in action? As we listen to Amanda attempt to engage Tyler, what suggestions might we give her as the conversation unfolds?

Timing. When to have the discussion is perhaps the most important decision. If Amanda and Tyler try to talk about it too soon they'll simply fall into old habits—Tyler will be frustrated by Amanda's hesitancy, while she'll feel disregarded. For now, perhaps the first step for Amanda is to acknowledge the importance of this issue to Tyler and his desire to talk. In the days before the conversation Amanda will need time to emotionally and spiritually prepare. If she doesn't, her powerful emotions will surely bleed into the conversation.

Intrapersonal perception and relational history. When heading into difficult conversations, we cannot ignore our self-talk. Our intrapersonal perceptions greatly impact how we react to others. Amanda's internal assessment of the situation might sound like this:

In today's difficult and uncertain economy, I am increasingly worried about our finances. Not only is it getting harder to make Tyler's paycheck stretch to meet our needs, we are setting aside zero money for our children's education or our retirement. We need to tighten the reins of the budget, not recklessly give to a problem half a world away! If we don't tighten things up now, what will be the result? Will we have to go into debt to send the kids to college? Will I have to go back to work? I love staying home and the kids need me during these early years. I also want to live a life of faith, but not at the expense of my family.

What Tyler sees as stepping out in faith Amanda views as reckless. Their relational history seems to be filled with a demand-withdrawal pattern where the more Tyler wants to give the more Amanda retreats, prompting Tyler to pursue even more, thus causing her to retreat further. Before she engages Tyler, it would be helpful for Amanda to identify what is fueling this recurring conflict. Two possible factors are at play.

First, Amanda may be feeling that a relational transgression has occurred. Specifically, she feels that Tyler is not privileging the relationship. In any significant relationship we assume that each person will give priority to the other person. From Amanda's perspective, Tyler seems to be putting his desires above her fears and concern for the family. Second, fears about finances are producing surging emotions, causing Amanda to become defensive whenever Tyler wants to discuss responding to other people's needs. In order to have a productive conversation, Amanda will need to address these emotions before sitting down with Tyler to talk.

Spiritual disciplines. In the coming days it will be important for Amanda to engage in a spiritual discipline that specifically addresses her concerns. Over the years, Amanda may have gradually assumed responsibility for making sure the family was taken care of financially. Carrying this burden entails counting every penny, resulting in increasingly anxious thoughts. *Will the economy ever recover? How long can our savings keep being depleted? Our investments haven't shown a positive return in years. What happens when the kids go off to college? Is it inevitable that I'll have to go back to work?* While these are legitimate questions, they can easily dominate her self-talk, resulting in a defensive posture toward Tyler and, perhaps, even God.

"Do not be anxious about anything," declares the apostle Paul to a young struggling church at Philippi (Phil 4:6). Rather, he suggests, approach all concerns with an attitude of prayer and thanksgiving. While concerns about finances are certainly understandable, Amanda may need to reflect on how much she has allowed herself to be consumed by them. Confession, notes Christian author Adele Calhoun, "means we open the bad in our lives to God."[1] During times of meditation and prayer Amanda may wrestle with the following questions: *As I struggle to trust Tyler with our finances, is it possible I also struggle to trust God? Is my first impulse to worry and take control or to bring my worries to God? Has God taken care of my family in the past? Do I trust God to speak to my husband about finances? Ultimately, is God able to provide?*

Amanda's anxiousness about finances, while understandable in these difficult times, needs to be brought to God. Confessing doubts about God's provision and meditating on his faithfulness will not only help settle her emotions, it may open the door to exploring Tyler's perspective. Perhaps it would be wise for Amanda to memorize Pauls' advice: "Do not be anxious about anything, but in every situation, by prayer . . . " (Phil 4:6). She simply cannot white-knuckle these emotions away. What distinguishes a Christian communicator from others is asking God to provide power to manage emotions.

As the conversation unfolds, Amanda attempts to work through the four questions we've been considering.

QUESTION ONE: WHAT DOES THIS PERSON BELIEVE?

The first step in a conversation is to listen to understand, not to evaluate. Seldom do people get defensive if we're seeking to better understand their perspective. What does Tyler believe about the pastor's call to give? While listening to Tyler's answer, Amanda will need to resist the urge to challenge statements he makes or correct what she deems are wrong or unfair assumptions. The time to present her view will come later in the conversation. For now, regardless of what Tyler says, Amanda must resist defensiveness. Let's listen as Amanda starts the conversation.

AMANDA: I know you were moved by the pastor's suggestion that we give to this missionary trying to help women escape sex trafficking. I was moved, too. What do you want to do?

TYLER: I want to give. God has blessed us with two beautiful children, my job and this house. I can't stand the thought of kids—many of them the age of our girls— trapped in such ugliness. If we take a step of faith and give to this project, God will honor it. Yes, it entails risk, but I know God will bless us!

AMANDA: How much do you think we should give?

TYLER: I've been thinking about it and I keep feeling like God is leading us to do something dramatic. I think we should give a couple of thousand to make sure the missionary gets those buildings. Will you at least think about it?

After hearing Tyler's perspective, we can easily see how defensiveness could creep into the conversation. Imagine if you were considering giving hundreds and your spouse suggested thousands. This is a crucial moment in the conversation. Amanda can continue to listen or abandon understanding and react defensively.

Communication tends to operate according to a cause-and-effect pattern in which one response provokes another. If Amanda puts her foot down, Tyler will react by putting his down as well. Now is the time for Amanda to ask God to calm her sense of panic and help stay engaged—"Do not be anxious about anything, but in every situation, by prayer . . ." Perhaps she could ask Tyler to explain what it would look like to give such a significant amount. Where does he envision the money coming from? Only when Amanda feels like she understands Tyler's perspective should she move on to the next question: Why does he want to give so much?

QUESTION TWO: WHY DOES HE BELIEVE IT?

Each person's point of view is the result of key individuals and experiences that have shaped his or her perspective. It is crucial that we uncover those influences. Amanda could continue the conversation by asking Tyler to describe how his desire to help others became such a conviction. As she listens, it will be important to look for a poetic moment where his passion crystallizes for her.

AMANDA: I admire you for wanting to help this missionary. Why do you think it's so important to you?

TYLER: I've always believed that faith is an action word.

AMANDA: What do you mean?

TYLER: Do you remember that men's conference I attended a few years ago with the guys in my Bible study?

AMANDA: You said it was pretty amazing.

TYLER: One of the speakers said something I'll never forget. "Men act on their faith! This is what separates the men from the boys!" Living by faith means you don't focus on circumstances. You focus on God. I want to be a man of God. I'm tired of cultural Christianity where what you hear on Sunday makes no difference in how you live during the week.

AMANDA: What do think it would it look like for you to walk by faith?

TYLER: It would mean going out on a limb for God. Do you remember my college roommate, Marcus? After he graduated he became a home contractor in Ohio. At the height of his business God told him to take a year off and build an orphanage. An entire year! And he did it! He cleaned out his savings and built it. I know it sounds crazy. Part of me thinks it was. Part of me greatly admires him.

AMANDA: How is he doing financially now? Did he ever recover his savings?

TYLER: He's not out of the woods yet, but he's slowly building his business and savings back up. He has a ways to go.

AMANDA: Is he married?

TYLER: Yeah (laughing). She almost divorced him. Not really. They both signed off on it.

No doubt each of Tyler's responses could be seen as a verbal shot across the bow. It would be easy for Amanda to react to his pointed implication that his contractor friend had a wife who supported him. And she can think of a million reasons why she and Tyler are in a totally different situation. In the heat of the moment it's crucial to remember that the purpose of step two is to engage in perspective taking—seeing the world through Tyler's eyes. Specifically, Amanda's goal is to form a complex view of him and cultivate empathy.

Developing a complex view of Tyler will require her to answer a few questions. First, how elaborate is her interpretation of Tyler's desire to give? If she has only one explanation—that he cares more about giving to a missionary than being financially responsible—then her view of him is limited and her response predictable. Can she think of other possibilities? Perhaps his heart is broken at the thought of young girls caught in the sex trade. Is he trying to impress the pastor or other men in his study? Is he living in the shadow of his college roommate? Or is it possible the Spirit is prompting him to take a step of faith? Most importantly, does Amanda notice any contradictory information that challenges her current view of Tyler? For example, is he financially responsible in other areas? Does he regularly bring up radical requests to give or is this a rarity? In the midst of an argument it's easy to adopt a view of a person that you are sure is correct. Asking these questions helps us form a thick, not thin, view of another.

> AMANDA: Two thousand dollars is a lot of money. I'm not saying this isn't worth it, but that amount is a lot.
>
> TYLER: Amanda, I know it's a lot.
>
> AMANDA: Can you help me understand why this issue has so captured your attention?
>
> TYLER: I can't fully explain it. I think it is has to do with our girls. I can't stop thinking about girls, the same age as ours, being forced to do such horrible things. What hope do they have? We can be that hope. What if no one responds and the buildings are sold to someone else? That would be tough to swallow. It would make me pretty angry.

Translation: it would make Tyler angry with Amanda if the buildings were lost. Again, now is not the time for Amanda to respond. Rather, she should seek to foster empathy. In this case, empathy is Amanda's attempt to project herself into Tyler's point of view in order to experience his thoughts and feelings. The following questions might be useful to consider: *What if I was in Tyler's position? Imagine feeling deeply stirred by the pastor's request to give. I have a chance to act like my college roommate and courageously follow God. Yet I know my wife will not support me. Instead of being excited, she'll try to talk me out of giving. How would I feel?* Remember, compassion is not condoning. Amanda needs to acknowledge Tyler's frustrations, which will set an empathetic tone to the conversation.

AMANDA: Tyler, I also couldn't bear the thought of our girls living like that with no one to help them. I didn't know you felt this deeply about it.

TYLER: I do.

AMANDA: It must be frustrating to feel so strongly about an issue and not have my support. If I were you, it would make me sad to feel alone in this.

TYLER: It is what it is.

As Amanda listened to Tyler, did she pick up on a poetic moment? Was there a phrase where she clearly sensed his passion or motivation? As you read this exchange, did you detect a poetic moment? For example, what did Tyler mean when he said acting on faith is what separates the men from the boys? How is giving to this cause possibly linked to his masculinity? Will he feel like less of a man for not giving? One gender theorist notes that if women are sex objects, men are success objects. Men often base their self-esteem on how successfully they complete tasks. Is it possible Tyler would view himself a failure as an authentic follower of God if he didn't respond dramatically to the challenge of securing these buildings? Without challenging him, Amanda should seek to gain clarification.

QUESTION THREE: WHERE DO WE AGREE?

Before Amanda presents her position to Tyler, it's imperative that she ask where she and Tyler agree. "Well," you may be thinking, "what if she doesn't agree with him? Yes, it's helpful for her to see this issue through his eyes, but there's no way she'll ever believe they can give thousands to this cause." Keep in mind that finding common ground does not mean she is agreeing to give Tyler's amount come Sunday.

Could Amanda cultivate common ground by focusing on the question and not on their differing answers? For example, as a couple, how might they respond to those caught in the sex trade? By focusing on the question she is affirming and agreeing that this tragic issue needs a response. By asking this question she is communicating that they both value social justice. What else about Tyler does she value? Is it important to walk in faith and be open to God's leading? Does she value a husband who wants to be a man of faith?

> AMANDA: I'll be honest; giving thousands to this cause is
>   scary to me.
> TYLER: I didn't think you'd go for it. This isn't the first time.
> AMANDA: I know. I worry about our finances. Maybe I worry
>   too much.
> TYLER: I'm not saying we should bust the bank. But I do
>   think we should step out in faith and give.
> AMANDA: I know you do. I was deeply moved by what the
>   pastor said and it breaks my heart to think of those
>   girls not having a place to live. I agree we need to do
>   something and I'm glad you are taking the lead on this.
>   I'm just not sure how much to give. But I am sure that
>   this issue is worth discussing how to respond.

A prerequisite to fostering common ground is a sense of humility and open-mindedness. Is Amanda open to Tyler's suggestion? Is it possible that God is leading her through him to radically give beyond her perceived means? If she wants Tyler to be open to her suggestions, then she must be open to his. If she wants him to cultivate areas of common ground with her, then she must do so first. God has made it clear that what we sow—openness, empathy, common ground—we will ultimately reap (Gal 6:7).

QUESTION FOUR: BASED ON ALL I'VE LEARNED, HOW SHOULD I PROCEED?

After listening, seeking to understand, and finding common ground, it's Amanda's turn to speak. What should she say? When crafting a response it's helpful to ask a key question: With this person, at this time, under these circumstances, what is the one thing I should say? Prioritizing becomes easier for Amanda if she asks other salient questions: *What is my history with Tyler? Do I regularly find myself at odds with his desire to give? When we disagree, how do our conversations go?* If they are filled with anger, raised voices or silence that seems to linger for days, then they have a negative history. In light of her answers Amanda may want to address the way they communicate rather than resolving this one issue. Since there is a deadline to their decision, circumstances dictate that they must make a decision in the next week or so. However, some issues simply cannot be resolved in a single conversation.

In light of this, what is the one thing Amanda should say to Tyler presently? Most individuals attempt to tackle an issue without a clear goal. Person-centered communication requires us to craft a response to a specific person and circumstance. If Amanda's communication with Tyler is poor when discussing finances, then she may want to address the relationship rather than the topic. For instance, when seeking areas of common ground with Tyler, Amanda noted that while she disagreed with the amount, she was pleased to have a husband who wanted to respond and step out by faith. Has she told him that? If she hasn't, then she may want that to be the one thing to say. Therefore, Amanda's agenda for this conversation is to acknowledge—a crucial part of a communication climate—that she is proud of him.

> AMANDA: I know we are in the middle of a disagreement, but there's something I want to say. Listening to you talk about your desire to help others and take steps of faith to do so really encourages me. You not only try to listen to God, but you are committed to following him. I admire that.
>
> TYLER: Thanks. That means a lot. So, what are we going to do?

While Amanda feels good that she has affirmed her husband, they still haven't settled the issue! The ache Amanda feels in the pit of her stomach and pervading anxiousness necessitates her continuing the disciplines of meditation and confession. God will, regardless of their decision, be committed to taking care of them. Amanda cannot let her fluctuating emotions cause her to abandon person-centered communication. Affirming Tyler was crucial and will set the tone for the next conversation. What Amanda needs now is time to process.

> AMANDA: I need some time to think about what you've said. Am I willing to follow God, even if that means stretching me out of my comfort zone? How do we balance family and giving by faith? I need to think and pray. Can we talk in a few days?

When the time comes to continue this conversation, Amanda will need to select a new goal. Since the deadline for the decision is near, she'll need to select a topic goal: how much are they going to give? While it was wise to postpone talking about the exact amount until Amanda gathered more information and affirmed Tyler, she can put off the decision only so long before it seems like she's evading the issue. While she knows the amount Tyler feels the Lord is leading him to give, what does she think?

As she responds, it will be helpful to keep several principles in mind. First, she needs to begin the conversation with a summary of where she and Tyler stand, giving equal weight to each position. She'll have to be careful not to skew the description to favor her point of view. If an impartial observer described their differing positions, what would he or she say?

> AMANDA: As I see it, we both feel led to help this missionary. It's horrible to think of these girls forced into sex trafficking and we both admire the missionary's attempt to secure these houses. Tyler, you feel led to give an amount that will stretch you, while I feel led to give an amount that stretches me. We agree on the cause, but disagree on the amount. Is that a fair summary?

It is imperative that Amanda's description be fair and one that Tyler can agree with. Now is not the time for Amanda to slip in a backhanded jab trying to position herself as the reasonable one or the only one looking out for the family.

Second, Amanda shouldn't shy away from letting Tyler know that she disagrees with the amount he is proposing. An honest response is like a kiss from a trusted friend. If she doesn't express how she feels, latent conflict will take root. She should also be careful not to preface a response by saying, "I know you'll be disappointed with the amount I want to give, but . . . " Research shows that using verbal hedges such as "I hope you won't get angry" or "Don't take this the wrong way" puts the receiver on the defense because you assume to know what he or she is thinking and how he or she will respond.[2] While avoiding the pitfall of being hyper-authentic or brutally real, Amanda should simply let Tyler know why she disagrees.

Third, seek to form a compromise. The word "compromise" comes from a Latin word meaning "middle way." Seeking to move to the middle entails both of them leaving entrenched positions to adopt a resolution both can support. Amanda can let Tyler know she is working toward compromise by telling him both what she'd like to give if it were solely up to her and what she is willing to consider.

> AMANDA: If I were making the decision, I'd give $500.
> Considering our finances that would be a step of faith.
> However, after hearing how strongly you feel about
> this issue and your desire to take an even greater step
> of faith, I'd be willing to consider more. It would
> stretch me, but I'm willing to trust God.

By voicing her willingness to compromise and move out of her comfort level she is utilizing the rule of reciprocation. Amanda's move toward Tyler creates pressure for him to reciprocate and move toward her. She's not trying to manipulate him but allowing him access to her thought process, seeing how he has influenced her. Tyler's move toward Amanda may not be enough (he may want to give $1,500), but at least they are considering each other's requests and moving from entrenched positions.

Also keep in mind that every compromise involves creativity. For example, if Tyler feels strongly that they should give a significant amount, what are some creative ways of finding extra income? Would Tyler be willing to work overtime to make money to give away? Could the family do a yard sale to raise extra money or do other types of fundraising? It's crucial for Amanda and Tyler to move away from seeing each other as the problem and to recast the problem as: how do we raise money for this worthwhile cause?

Last, Amanda may need to allow Tyler to save face (identity goal) as he considers giving a lesser amount. What if he's already told his friends about his desire to radically respond? What separates the men from the boys is living by faith. How can he go back and explain to his friends he is giving half of what he said?

> AMANDA: I know that if it weren't for me, you'd graciously
> give a significant amount. Taking my reservations and

fears into consideration, would you be willing to give less than what you want? I'm willing to step out in faith, but I need your help.

What if Amanda and Tyler still can't reach a compromise? What if Tyler stays firm to giving the full amount? The Scriptures are clear that we live in community and should lean on each other during trying times. If no compromise can be secured, then it may be time to bring in a third party to help give perspective. Just as early followers would argue their case at the city gate in front of local leaders, Tyler and Amanda may need to have this discussion under the guidance of a trained pastor or trusted layperson who can moderate from a neutral position.

The good news about marital conflict is that research suggests that if handled properly, disagreements can ultimately strengthen a relationship and foster feelings of togetherness, resulting in more productive conversations in the future.[3]

Case Study Two

Disagreeing over
Religion in the Workplace

When we're growing up, we soon learn there are two topics we should avoid talking about at all costs: politics and religion. Discussing these topics is certain to produce defensiveness and raised voices. This puts Christians interested in presenting the Christian perspective to others in a difficult situation, particularly if we want to share with coworkers. What if bringing up Christianity causes conflict or tension? We often wrestle with two competing desires—fitting in with the organizational culture and representing Christ. In the following scenario we follow Terrance, who wants to share his faith with a Muslim coworker through implementing our strategy. How can he represent the Christian worldview without offending or causing a rift?

SETUP

Terrance and Ahmed work together at a midsize company in Dearborn, Michigan. The company is ethnically diverse and reflects the large Muslim community in Dearborn. More than seven million

Muslims are living in the United States with Dearborn having the largest concentration of Arab Muslims in North America. Over the past year they have joked about sports, the challenge of raising teenagers, and company-related issues. One common area of interest is faith. Terrance is an evangelical Christian while Ahmed is Muslim. But they have talked about religion only in generalities: how to pass on religious values to teenagers, maintain a sense of spirituality within a hectic schedule, and so on.

Terrance increasingly feels guilty about not sharing his faith with Ahmed. He takes seriously the Scriptures' description of Christians as "Christ's ambassadors" who have been entrusted with the "message of reconciliation" (2 Cor 5:19-20). Their discussion about religion seems to touch only the surface. Terrance decides to take a risk and asks Ahmed if he'd like to grab lunch next week so he can hear more about the specifics of Islam. As he heads into this meeting, what advice can we offer him?

Timing. Terrance has done a great job in creating a healthy communication climate and a positive relational history with Ahmed. It is a relationship built on commonalities—parenting, faith, spirituality—and now Terrance wants to discuss Christianity specifically. Yet what is his motivation for doing so? Is it feelings of guilt for not doing it sooner or a genuine concern for Ahmed and a sense that the timing is right? Relieving feelings of guilt will put the focus on Terrance, while concern for Ahmed will keep the conversation person-centered.

Intrapersonal perception. As in any conversation, being aware of self-talk is vital. What is Terrance's assessment of his relationship with Ahmed as their lunch approaches?

Every time I've thought about questioning Ahmed's worldview or sharing my faith I psych myself out. I constantly hear people describe Christians as judgmental and intolerant. What if I come across as judgmental? What if Ahmed is offended by what I believe? My pastor once said in a sermon, "Only the fear of God will deliver you from the fear

of man!" Do I care what God thinks of me or Ahmed? Am I more con-
cerned with his soul or our working relationship? Yet what if the con-
versation goes badly and there's a rift between us? This conversation
could have a dramatic impact on my ability to work with him and do
my job. Religious disagreements causing tension will not sit well with
our manager. Part of me just wants to have the conversation and be
done with it.

Terrance's fears are legitimate. If not dealt with they will, like
some type of emotional contagion, be transferred onto Ahmed. He
will, perhaps even subconsciously, pick up on Terrance's uneasiness
and react accordingly. Sadly, many Christians communicate in a
way that is dismissive and intolerant. But is that Terrance?

The difficulty is that Terrance is reacting to a conversation that
hasn't happened yet. As he imagines talking to Ahmed about the
gospel, he envisions it going badly. One of the most difficult conversations we can have is the one we imagine. As the lunch draws
near Terrance will have to remind himself that his strong communication climate and relational history with Ahmed are positive
factors. Hopefully their climate will grow even stronger as Terrance
begins the conversation by listening, seeking to understand, and
finding common ground—the first three steps of our method.

Evangelism is a process, not a one-time event. All the time
spent cultivating a relationship with Ahmed is what apologists call
"pre-evangelism." Terrance needs to resist the pull of agenda
anxiety, which is the temptation to have the entire conversation
at once. Working together affords them the opportunity to continue the conversation in the weeks ahead. It will do no good to
force the conversation.

Spiritual disciplines. In today's culture "proselytizing" has
become a dirty word, and it's understandable that Terrance is concerned about offending a coworker. Tensions within the workplace
are not to be taken lightly. It seems that Terrance is concerned about
coming across as judgmental. What spiritual discipline would be

beneficial in addressing that fear? It may be helpful to engage in the discipline of worship as Terrance prepares for the conversation. Worship is the act of redirecting our focus toward God and acknowledging who he is and what he can do.

One of the central attributes of God found in the Scriptures is love. When the apostle John describes God, he doesn't say that God is a lover; he says he is love (1 Jn 4:8). In receiving his love we "become children of God" (Jn 1:12). It is this love Terrance is offering Ahmed. He is offering him the opportunity to enter a relationship in which all past, present and future failures are forgiven. God's love is transcendent and removes all fear (1 Jn 4:18). We don't have to work hard to keep his love or impress him. Sure, what Terrance is advocating runs counter to key aspects of a works-based religion like Islam and may elicit a defensive reaction from Ahmed. Yet at the heart of Terrance's message is an invitation to enter a divine relationship rooted in security and love. It has changed his life and he wants to make it available to Ahmed. Where's the offense in that?

Penn Jillette, illusionist and outspoken atheist, was flattered rather than offended when an audience member handed him a Gideon Bible. In his video blog he commented that if a person believed he had a relationship with God that had transformed his life and ensured escaping judgment, "how much would you have to hate me to not tell me?"[1] Rather than viewing his desire to share his faith with Ahmed as being something that will offend, Terrance should view it as an opportunity to show genuine concern. How much would he have to hate Ahmed not to tell him about a relationship that had transformed him? Terrance's fear that his delivery will seem judgmental or intolerant will be alleviated as he works through the four questions of our method, which starts with listening.

QUESTION ONE: WHAT DOES THIS PERSON BELIEVE?

While Terrance may have a general knowledge of Islam, this upcoming lunch will be an opportunity to hear about it from Ahmed's perspective. And his version may not exactly follow the tenets of orthodox Islam. Like many today, Ahmed might have his own unique version of a faith tradition. Terrance's goal is to uncover what Islam means to Ahmed, not how it corresponds exactly with traditional beliefs.

TERRANCE: I've always enjoyed our discussions about the importance of faith and how it helps us cope with life, work and teenagers.

AHMED: Me too. Except it doesn't seem to help much with teens!

TERRANCE: (Laughing.) Agreed. While I know a little about your faith, I'd like to know more. How would you describe Islam? What attracts you to it?

AHMED: To me, Islam is a religion of peace. We are mainly concerned with cultivating peace with God and others. The Quran teaches that peace is one of the names of Allah and many Muslims end their daily worship with the simple prayer "O God, you are Peace."

Terrance may be surprised by Ahmed's answer. He's heard the opposite about Islam. Terrance's friends describe it as a violent religion that suppresses women, persecutes other faiths and believes in jihad, or holy war. What preconceived notions of Islam did he carry into the conversation? It will be helpful for him to set them aside and allow Ahmed to define Islam for himself.

TERRANCE: How do you cultivate peace with God?

AHMED: While most of us desire God, we often lose our way or get distracted. Muslims believe that all people, deep down, are good at heart. We just have a tendency to mess up due to lack of information or negative influences. Knowing this, God sends us rules that are meant to guide us back to him. These rules come through leaders—you could call them pastors, we call

them imams. Of course, the clearest descriptions of
these rules come through the Quran.[2]

TERRANCE: What are some of these rules?

AHMED: There are five broad rules, which we think of as pillars.
These pillars focus on prayer, fasting, giving to the poor,
traveling to holy sites and reciting a simple creed: "There
is no God but Allah, and Muhammad is the messenger
of God." All of our rules can be summarized by one
word—submission. You may not know, but the word
"Islam" means "submission." If we follow these rules, we
will prosper in this life and the life to come.

Our devotion to Christ often makes us poor listeners. When we
hear a claim that contradicts our faith, we feel compelled to respond
immediately. Now is not the time for Terrance to challenge; rather,
he needs to continue to understand Islam and create a cognitively
complex picture of Ahmed. Allowing him the freedom to speak
uninterrupted is deeply affirming.

TERRANCE: Tell me about some of these rules.

AHMED: Sure. Giving is important because everything
belongs to Allah. He has merely entrusted me with
money and possessions so I can give to others. We
refer to giving as *zakah*, which means purification. As I
give to others I am in turn purified before God.

TERRANCE: What else?

AHMED: This may not be appropriate to talk about at lunch,
but we also practice fasting.

TERRANCE: (With mouth full.) Sorry, what did you say?

AHMED: (Laughing.) Don't worry, we mostly only fast during
the month of Ramadan.

TERRANCE: You fast for a whole month?

AHMED: Yes, from dawn until sundown we abstain from food,
drink and even sex. When we give up these things we

are developing, like a muscle, self-restraint. In a culture where people gorge themselves on food and sex, we want to cultivate control. I'm not saying it's fun or that I even always do it. But it's an important part of my faith.

As Terrance listens, there are issues he'd like for Ahmed to elaborate on. While Ahmed says he supports the idea of fasting, he mentioned he doesn't always do it.

TERRANCE: Are there people who don't want to or can't follow the rules? What then?

AHMED: Well, it happens. I'd be the first to admit that I'm not always as consistent as I'd want to be.

TERRANCE: Ditto.

AHMED: God treats us as adults. He tells us what to do and reminds us that we are capable of following his rules. If we don't, then there is no one to blame but ourselves. As a parent you lay out family rules and make known the rewards or consequences for following or disregarding them. You also let them know that you think they are good kids and encourage them to be obedient. But, ultimately, it's their choice. That is how God treats us. In the Quran there are verses that scare me and also bring comfort. One verse describes God sitting before a set of scales that weigh our good and bad actions. If the bad outweigh the good, judgment is certain.[3] Yet I don't despair because Allah is merciful. Almost every chapter, or *surah*, of the Quran starts with the phrase "In the name of Allah, the merciful and compassionate." I take comfort in such reminders.

TERRANCE: What if the scale tips in the wrong direction? Do Muslims believe in hell?

AHMED: Yes. Hell is portrayed as a place of pain and even torture.

TERRANCE: Doesn't sound fun.

AHMED: No. Not at all.

Ahmed has given Terrance much to think about. It's becoming obvious that Islam's approach to salvation is based on following rules and hoping that the scales tip in your favor. Terrance may be tempted to ditch the next steps of our method in order to present a Christian approach to salvation rooted in grace. Yet there are three more steps that will help Terrance in formulating a response.

QUESTION TWO: WHY DOES HE BELIEVE THIS?

When asking this question Terrance's goal is to form a complex, or thick, description of Ahmed.

TERRANCE: Why is it important to you that people understand Islam as a religion of peace?

AHMED: Do you remember a couple of years ago the shooting rampage at Fort Hood, Texas?

TERRANCE: Vaguely. Didn't it involve a Muslim solider shooting fellow soldiers?

AHMED: Yes, and that's my point. The shooter was a soldier of Arab descent who handed out Qurans leading up to the attack and shouted, "Allah Akbar"—God is great—as he shot and killed thirteen soldiers. It was a tragic incident involving an unstable man. Equally tragic was the reaction. After the attack someone left a hardbound copy of the Quran at the doorstep of my mosque. It had been defaced with spray paint. Inside was a note that read, "Islam is a disease. Muslim immigrants are the virus. Every Muslim should be kicked out of the USA."[4]

TERRANCE: That's crazy.

AHMED: I know that such talk should be ignored. But it's hard to do. Did you know that right after the bombing of the federal building in Oklahoma City news outlets quickly reported that suspicious Middle Eastern individuals had been seen in the area before the bombing? Of course, later we learned that it was Midwestern Caucasians who were responsible. People think that all Arabs are Muslims and all Muslims are violent. It's very frustrating. We are a religion of peace, but people think we are violent. As an Arab living in the States, when you are listening to the news and hear of a shooting or bombing your first thought is often: God, don't let the shooter be a Muslim.

All of our perspectives have been shaped by significant experiences. How have events like the Fort Hood shooting and 9/11 shaped Ahmed's desire to have people view his religion as one of peace? How would Terrance feel if people only associated Christianity with the Crusades or violent acts done by unstable individuals in the name of Christ? A key component of cognitive complexity is to understand the psychological reasons why individuals act as they do.

The Fort Hood shooting and the angry reaction to it offered Terrance a glimpse into why Ahmed wants to present Islam as a peaceful worldview. As he listens, does he detect a poetic moment in which Ahmed's passion or emotions surface? For example, how angry would Terrance be if after a violent event he discovered a defaced Bible left at his church blaming Christianity and calling it a disease? As the conversation continues, is there still need for clarification?

TERRANCE: Can I ask about jihad? I know the concept is
            controversial, but I don't know much about it. What is
            it and do you support it?

AHMED: Yes, I do. Jihad is a Muslim's belief in holy war.
            However, let me say two things about it. First, not all

Muslim theologians agree on what the Quran teaches about this topic. You are a Christian. Not all Christian scholars or pastors agree on every doctrine or passage of the Bible, do they?

TERRANCE: Uh, no. We have plenty of lively and heated disagreements.

AHMED: Well, we do, too. It's impossible to boil all of the richness and diversity of Muslim perspectives into one monolithic voice. When it comes to a controversial idea like holy war, you are going to get very different ideas coming from the Muslim community. Second, most Muslims I know believe that when jihad was started by Muhammad it was done only as a form of self-defense. As I understand the Quran, it teaches that holy war should be waged only in defense of life and property and never to oppress or dominate another. So six days after the terrorist attacks of 9/11, dozens of leading Islamic scholars issued a statement that said they were grief-stricken at such horrifying events and the murder of innocents could never be justified nor tolerated by true followers of Islam. However, because the idea of jihad is so controversial, it's all people think of when it comes to Islam.

As Ahmed speaks it's obvious Terrance has hit a nerve. His reaction surfaces fears within Terrance that he might be seen as judgmental and the relationship will suffer. It's important for Terrance to remind himself that he is only gathering information and attempting to form a thick impression of Ahmed and his faith. Ultimately, he is offering Ahmed a chance to enter into a relationship with a God who is love and wants to love him. Meditating on this during the conversation will give him perspective and a sense that God is involved as they talk.

QUESTION THREE: WHERE DO WE AGREE?

At this point in the conversation, Terrance has a decision to make. Does he challenge the parts of Islam he disagrees with, or does he focus on areas of agreement? Remember Paul's approach while surrounded by idols in Athens. Instead of attacking idol worship, he described the idols as "objects of worship." Can Terrance do the same? Are there any areas of overlap between how Ahmed and Terrance seek to live out or practice their beliefs?

> TERRANCE: As I listen to you I'm amazed how much we value similar things. For Christians giving to the poor is an important part of worship. The Bible even says that if I see a person in need and don't respond, the love of God is not active in me. The same is true with fasting. I can't say I fast as often as I should, but the Bible is clear that it's a key way to learn how to focus on God.

Affirming an aspect of a person's faith tradition doesn't mean affirming the entire tradition. In addition to specific practices, are there common values Terrance can affirm?

> TERRANCE: I keep thinking back to what you said about the person defacing the Quran and leaving it outside your mosque. That was wrong. I can't imagine how I'd feel if someone started ripping up the Bible I keep in my desk. I got upset once when I spilled some coffee on a page.
>
> AHMED: To purposefully deface the Quran is awful. Do you know that if a Quran is accidentally dropped on the ground and damaged it must be carefully and respectfully destroyed?[5]
>
> TERRANCE: I admire that. Unfortunately, Christians often own so many Bibles that if we misplace one, we simply grab another. Most Bibles have the word "holy" on the cover, but I don't think we treat them that way. It

would do us well to adopt your take on how to handle something we consider sacred.

Terrance not only acknowledges aspects of how Ahmed practices his faith but affirms how he can learn from it. Going the extra mile in acknowledging and even learning from key aspects of Ahmed's faith will cultivate in Ahmed an openness to learn from Terrance.

QUESTION FOUR: BASED ON ALL I'VE LEARNED, HOW SHOULD I PROCEED?

Now that it's Terrance's turn to speak, what will he say? In answering this question Terrance adopts a person-centered approach that asks, "With this person, at this time, under these circumstances, what is the one thing I should say?" The two coworkers have been talking for a while and soon lunch will be over. What goal should Terrance adopt? It depends on how Terrance thinks the conversation is going. If he thinks it's going poorly, or Ahmed is increasingly growing defensive, then he may want to select a relational goal and buttress the communication climate. If it's been positive, then perhaps he could select a topic goal that addresses a specific issue.

In the last fifteen minutes before lunch ends, what does Terrance want Ahmed to think about? In light of the time restraints, it may be wise for him merely to bring up a topic for Ahmed to think about in preparation for a future discussion. Just as Ahmed wanted Terrance to know that Islam is a religion of peace, what does Terrance want him to know about Christianity? Is there an aspect of Christianity that is not only central but will cause Ahmed to evaluate Islam in light of it?

TERRANCE: As I listen to you describe your faith it is interesting how Christians also want peace with God and how rules help us obey him. These rules or guidelines help us prioritize life and live in obedience.

I think what is different between our faith traditions is what happens when we don't follow these rules.

AHMED: What do you mean?

TERRANCE: Have you ever gone through a period in your walk with God where you didn't do so well?

AHMED: Regrettably, yes.

TERRANCE: There was a time in college when I walked away from God and didn't want anything to do with him or his rules. This period lasted for years. And even today, I often have good and bad days following through on my Christian convictions. If what you say is true and God is placing my good and bad actions on a scale, I'd hate to think in what direction it is now tipping. How long would it take to counteract my disobedience? How could I know when I've broken even or created a positive balance?

AHMED: Well, all we can do is our best and hope for God's mercy.

TERRANCE: But what if you could be certain of the outcome? If you knew in advance that all the bad was dealt with and forgiven? We still seek to be obedient of God's guidelines, but we never doubt where we stand with him. At the heart of my faith is the idea that we can know and experience God's forgiveness today. To be absolutely assured of a secure relationship with God.

AHMED: But if you knew all was forgiven, then how you live now is unimportant. If the kids already know the parents will forgive everything, then why not just break the rules they don't like? If there were no consequences, there would be no obedience.

Lunch is over and Terrance has interjected two powerful thoughts into the conversation. The first is what happens in the life of a believer when he or she goes through seasons of disobedience. How many acts of devotion does it take to overcome these lapses? Muslim scholars frequently debate how Allah weighs good and bad actions. Are they treated equally or does he give more weight to good actions? Are there some bad actions that forever tip the scale toward judgment? These theologians readily admit that the Quran is unclear on these questions. Second, Terrance has asked Ahmed to consider a different perspective where rules are important and obedience expected but God's love and forgiveness are assured. Ahmed's objection, that grace opens the door to disobedience, mirrors the apostle Paul's similar concern that grace can easily be abused (Rom 6:1). Terrance should affirm this observation and set up another time to talk.

TERRANCE: Your concern that being assured of God's forgiveness might temper motivation for obedience is spot on. The Bible agrees that such a belief might have negative consequences and addresses it in depth. Perhaps we can grab lunch in a week or so and I'll explain.

In following days it's crucial for Terrance to return to his normal exchanges with Ahmed of phatic, or everyday, communication. The temptation might be to now make every conversation about spiritual things or a comparison of Christianity and Islam. Remember, it is the small talk—sports, office jokes, deadlines, frustration with teens—that sets up the significant dialogue that will happen the next time they have lunch.

Case Study Three

Teens and Excessive Use
of Video Games

Xbox, PS3 and Wii.

If you have adolescents and a television or computer, you need no further explanation. Children spend more time sitting in front of electronic screens than any other activity besides sleeping.[1] And a significant amount of this time is spent in video gaming. Video gaming is different than merely passively watching television since players are brought into a script that rewards them for achieving certain skills and reaching new levels. With increased playing time come alarming consequences such as dependence on the high of playing, time distortion, diminished empathy, irritability, decreased family relationships and decline in school performance. Individuals who play violent video games such as Call of Duty or Assassin's Creed exhibit increased anger, fights with peers or family members, and primed aggressive thoughts.[2] An overdependence on video games can be so controlling it is sometimes referred to as a nonsubstance addiction.

In the following scenario, Gwenn, a single mom, is concerned about her son's declining grades and withdrawal from the family due to constant video game playing. She's just received Dwayne's high school progress report, which confirmed that his grades are slipping at an alarming rate. She's been reluctant to talk to him but feels compelled to intervene. How can our communication strategy help her?

SETUP

Since Gwenn's divorce, she's had to work full time. She knows she's gone too much, but bills have to be paid. While she leaves specific directions for her two boys (Miles is twelve; Dwayne is fifteen) explaining that homework should be completed before television or video games, she often feels ignored. Since the divorce Dwayne has isolated himself from her by spending most of his time in his room. She suspects that he spends the majority of that time on social media and playing video games. Gradually, Dwayne has become irritable and confrontational in his tone with her. Gwenn tries to give him space, but after receiving his progress report she feels like she must voice her concerns and set some new rules about electronics.

Timing. Like most high school students, Dwayne is keenly aware that progress reports have come out and that his grades have slipped even more. He wonders if she'll read him the riot act this time. Since the divorce, Gwenn has lost her nerve to discipline, but she also knows that based on Dwayne's grades they need to talk. While the grades need to be discussed, is their communication climate strong enough to support the conversation? Should she first work on rebuilding it? What aspect needs the most attention?

Perhaps the aspect of commitment needs attention. Since the divorce Dwayne has noticed that his mother seldom disciplines him like she did when his parents were married. It's possible that Dwayne perceives this lack of discipline as a lack of commitment to him. For this conversation to be productive, Gwenn needs to identify why she has been reluctant to hold him to her standards.

Intrapersonal perception. As Gwenn prepares to talk to her son about grades and his isolation, what are her thoughts and perceptions heading into it?

I'm frustrated and scared. Dwayne has so much potential and all he does is sit in his room for hours playing those stupid games! The only time I see him is when he comes out to get something to eat. Now, he's even started stashing food in his room so he won't have to come out. When I go to bed and ask if homework's done, I barely get a response. Since I have to get up early for work I can't wait until he finally falls asleep. I tell him to make sure it's finished and no playing games past midnight. When I go to bed I can see the glow of the screen coming out from under the door.

I also feel guilty. I know our divorce shook his and his brother's world. What credibility do I have to tell him to shape up since I'm the one who caused the damage? Maybe playing video games helps him cope. How can I take that away from him? Yet I have to talk to him! It's not just the grades—though they are a mess—but it's the kind of games he's playing. Just looking at the covers makes me sick. What possible pleasure can there be in killing people for fun? I thought I raised him to respect all that God created. Have I failed as a parent?

It's obvious that for Gwenn this issue surfaces powerful emotions. She's angry about the grades, she's scared at the behavior video games are producing, and she feels guilty about the lingering effects of her divorce. Before she can address her son, she needs to address these surging emotions. When she sees Dwayne she not only perceives his failings but her failings as well. If she were to have the conversation without addressing these emotions it would greatly hinder the conversation. While all of her emotions are powerful, it is imperative she identity the one or two that most color her perception of herself and her son. What emotion does she struggle with the most? Anger at Dwayne's gaming obsession and poor grades or fear that she's not a good mother? If she feels that she has forfeited her credibility because she's no longer with their father, then that issue needs to be addressed.

As you'll remember from our discussion of credibility, or ethos, Aristotle noted that virtue is paramount to being credible in the eyes of others. If Gwenn thinks she's compromised her ethos because she's divorced, then she'll either back away from confronting her son or be timid in her approach. Before having this conversation, she needs to enter into a time of spiritual preparation.

Spiritual disciplines. Gwenn is struggling with two issues. First, she's haunted by her failed marriage. Second, she lacks confidence to parent. Each needs to be dealt with through a spiritual discipline.

Confession is a time where we expose our failures to God in order to claim forgiveness. It would be wise for Gwenn to reflect, under the guidance of the Spirit, what she contributed to the troubles of the marriage. However, regardless of her role, she needs to embrace God's all-encompassing forgiveness. "If we confess our sins he is faithful and just and will forgive us our sins and purify us from all unrighteousness" (1 Jn 1:9). The word "purify" not only entails God reminding us that our sins are forgiven but his removal of any lingering guilt of past sins. Through the process of confession Gwenn can claim forgiveness and move on, confident in her relationship with God.

Meditating on the Scriptures allows us to understand what God has called us to as parents. The apostle Paul admonishes parents to raise children "in the training and instruction of the Lord" (Eph 6:4). The word "instruction" carries the idea of intentionally giving input and direction to children. God has called Gwenn, as a parent, to give direction to Dwayne. She can take comfort in knowing that the "one who calls you is faithful and he will do it" (1 Thess 5:24). Through meditation Gwenn can take confidence that God will be faithful to her as she faithfully instructs her children. Committing these verses to memory could be beneficial when doubts resurface. Deep-seated doubts and fears will take consistent practicing of spiritual disciplines to shape our self-talk and intrapersonal perceptions. After her confidence grows, Gwenn can start to think through how to utilize our strategy to engage and instruct Dwayne.

QUESTION ONE: WHAT DOES THIS PERSON BELIEVE?

Rather than merely offering her conclusions to Dwayne, it could be helpful for Gwenn to present the issue to him and hear his point of view. The goal is to understand what he thinks about his grades and the possible impact of video gaming.

GWENN: Last week your progress report came.

DWAYNE: OK.

GWENN: What do you think it said?

DWAYNE: I'm sure it wasn't pretty.

GWENN: Some classes were better than others, but all your grades have gone down.

DWAYNE: (Silence.)

GWENN: What's going on?

DWAYNE: Nothing. Don't need to make a big deal about it.

GWENN: It's a big deal, because you matter to me. Is everything OK?

DWAYNE: I'm fine.

GWENN: Dwayne, we need to talk about this. I don't just want to set up a bunch of rules or take things away from you.

DWAYNE: Then don't.

GWENN: Can I tell you what I think is causing problems?

DWAYNE: Do I have a choice?

GWENN: No. I suppose not. I wonder how much video games are interfering with your schoolwork.

DWAYNE: I knew that was coming! My games are not a problem. It's how I relax. I'm not the only one playing them. Everyone does.

Gwenn is frustrated at her son's defensiveness and minimal answers. So far, asking the first question of our strategy has produced predictable answers. Dwayne doesn't think video games are an issue, and she does. If Gwenn challenges his answers it will evoke an angry confrontation. Central to listening is forming a complex view of a person in which the listener tries to uncover psychological motivations for actions. Does Gwenn know much about Dwayne's interests? There are hundreds of games out there; which is his favorite?

GWENN: What video games?

DWAYNE: What?

GWENN: What video games do you like to play?

DWAYNE: Come on, mom. Just let me go. I'll even go study.

GWENN: Wow, you'll do anything not to have this conversation. What games? Is there a favorite?

DWAYNE: Seriously?

GWENN: Yeah, seriously.

DWAYNE: OK, Call of Duty: Black Ops.

GWENN: That's the war game, isn't it?

DWAYNE: Yeah, it's the war game. You've never seen it, have you? The visuals are great. The missions they send you on are crazy. It took me days to complete the missions.

GWENN: Days? How much sleep were you getting? Never mind homework.

DWAYNE: Yeah, I overdid it.

GWENN: What do you like best about it?

DWAYNE: Can I just go?

GWENN: Give me an answer and you can go. Go to study, I mean. (Smiling.)

DWAYNE: *Sigh*. There are levels to the game. The highest is prestige. When you reach that level you start the whole game over, but it's now insanely difficult. One mistake and you're killed. And there's always someone better than you online. There are some seriously good players out there.

GWENN: Are you one of them?

DWAYNE: That's another question. You said last one.

GWENN: You're right. Goodbye. I'll call you for dinner.

As Dwayne leaves Gwenn is oddly encouraged. That's the most they've talked in a while. She hates the violence of Call of Duty but noticed a slight glimmer of excitement when he spoke about it. What is it about this game that he finds so appealing? After dinner, she decides to ask.

QUESTION TWO: WHY DOES THIS PERSON BELIEVE THIS?

As they are doing the dishes Gwenn continues the conversation. Why is he so attracted to a game that is so violent? What has shaped his view of this game?

GWENN: Did you know that two of the top-selling video games this past year are FIFA 2014 and NBA 2K14?

DWAYNE: Where did you hear that?

GWENN: I have my sources.

DWAYNE: Internet?

GWENN: Internet. Why not one of those games? Something sports related?

DWAYNE: Do I look like the sports type?

GWENN: You did great at sports.

DWAYNE: Spoken like a mom. I sucked. Middle of the pack. Sometimes not even that.

GWENN: I didn't know you felt that way.

DWAYNE: It's true. Except in first-person shooter games I'm not middle of the pack.

GWENN: First-person—what?

DWAYNE: Get out much? In games like Call of Duty or Assassin's Creed, you control a person who defends and attacks others. I rock. Online shooters know not to mess with me.

GWENN: You play online?

DWAYNE: Online is where the real competition is. My friends
know I'm the one to have on your team!

GWENN: Have I met any of these kids?

DWAYNE: No. I haven't met them either. They're my online
friends.

Experiences deeply shape our view of others and ourselves. As
she listened Gwenn seemed genuinely surprised that Dwayne didn't
see himself as athletic. In a high school culture where jocks are held
in high esteem, it must have been painful to realize he was average
or even below average. With his grades tanking Dwayne must also
feel like an outsider to those who excel academically. So where does
he fit? Where is his self-esteem rooted? Are there any specific individuals who shaped his perspective?

GWENN: Who taught you how to play?

DWAYNE: You won't like it.

GWENN: Try me.

DWAYNE: Dad. When I go to his place, we play. He's pretty
good. Even before the split we played when you did
church things.

GWENN: I didn't know that.

DWAYNE: Are we done?

GWENN: (Nods.)

Gwenn is angry with her ex for encouraging Dwayne's video
gaming and mad at herself for being so busy she didn't know what
was going on. Her feelings of inadequacy could easily surface right
now and cause her to bail on future conversations. Meditating on
the Scripture's command to instruct Dwayne and being assured of
God's subsequent faithfulness can give Gwenn confidence to continue pursing Dwayne. As the anger subsides, she'll need to consider the valuable information she learned in this short exchange.

Did Gwenn detect a poetic moment while she listened? While

her son feels below average in most areas, he stated that when it comes to video games, online shooters know not to mess with me. His gaming community doesn't merely tolerate him but wants him on their team. It's a place where he finds value, acceptance and success. Gender theorists note that boys are often taught that to be masculine entails not just winning but being superior to others and setting oneself above the pack.[3] In most areas of his life—school or home—Dwayne is seen as trouble, or a problem to be fixed. In the gaming community he is a valued asset.

Gaming is also a way for Dwayne to connect with a father no longer in the home. His self-esteem is linked—for good or bad—to his father and friends. For Dwayne, gaming has become an entry point to both a community and an estranged father. Gaining this information does not mean Gwenn cannot or should not put limits on her son's gaming or restrict its content. However, utilizing the idea of feedforward, she needs to anticipate the impact her actions will have on Dwayne's community, self-esteem and relationship with his father. While she initially viewed his gaming as a form of entertainment, she now is coming to understand the much deeper value Dwayne attaches to it.

QUESTION THREE: WHERE DO WE AGREE?

At first, Gwenn is stumped trying to find areas of agreement with a violent video game. She is strongly at odds with the violence and language of first-person shooter games such as Call of Duty. Where can common ground be cultivated? Just as famed atheist Richard Dawkins didn't agree with the content of the King James Bible, he still saw value in having British school kids read great literary works of Western civilization.

Could the same be true of video games? If Gwenn temporarily overlooks the content, can she find value in playing? While researchers note the negative effects of gaming, they also point out positive outcomes, such as an increased self-confidence, problem solving and, most interestingly, the potential to bond with family members. Gwenn has a choice to make. She can view Call of Duty as something unredeemable or as something that has some valuable outcomes. She can either enter Dwayne's world or seek to shut it down.

Gwenn surprises the boys by stopping at Dwayne's favorite fast food joint on her way home from work. As any mom knows, the way to a man's heart is through his stomach. As they eat, she attempts to cultivate common ground.

GWENN: You were right; the graphics of Call of Duty are awesome.

DWAYNE: Where did you see Call of Duty?

GWENN: During my lunch break I went to the video store down the street. I asked the guy behind the counter to show it to me. He put it on the big screen.

DWAYNE: And?

GWENN: Remember, you're talking to a woman raised on Ms. Pac-Man. It was impressive. I wasn't thrilled with the cussing.

DWAYNE: They're just words.

GWENN: And I'm not thrilled with such a casual view of profanity. We can talk about that later. I asked him how hard the game is. He said if someone is playing at the prestige level, he or she has reached level fifty-five and has to be—to use his words—"wicked good." He said some players even go pro, get sponsors and make a living at it.

DWAYNE: I know. Love to beat one of those guys!

GWENN: I'm sure you could one day.

DWAYNE: Spoken like a mom.

GWENN: And a fan.

Visiting the video store was a decision to engage in perspective-taking with Dwayne. Going there does not mean she wholeheartedly endorses Call of Duty, but rather that she's attempting to enter Dwayne's world. They now have a common vocabulary and reference point. Her desire to understand her son has also enacted the rule of reciprocation where Gwenn's son may now be motivated to understand her. It also gives her an opportunity to bring up a subject that they often avoid.

> GWENN: It must be a cool thing to play with your father.
>
> DWAYNE: (Silence.)
>
> GWENN: I can't say I'm happy he didn't discuss it with me, but I can see how it would feel great to connect with him and show off how good you are. I wish we had something like that.
>
> DWAYNE: I have two controllers for Call of Duty.
>
> GWENN: I'm not there yet. How about going to the mall and shopping?
>
> DWAYNE: Not likely.
>
> GWENN: Can't blame a girl for trying.

QUESTION FOUR: BASED ON ALL I'VE LEARNED, HOW SHOULD I PROCEED?

While Gwenn has gathered valuable information and discovered pockets of common ground, Dwayne's grades are still slipping and he's spending too much time gaming. What should she do or say? That will depend on her goal for the next conversation. If she wants to discuss setting rules or issuing punishment, then she should adopt a topic goal. However, there may be a more significant issue at play. Relational goals ask the question "Who are we to each other?" The success of future conversations is determined by the answer to that question. In addition to the content level of communication, the relational level determines how much power and respect exist between speakers. The relational level cannot be ignored because it often carries "more urgency than topic interests."[4]

In the past Gwenn's self-talk has been riddled with self-doubt over her failed marriage. Does she have the credibility to speak into her son's life? Through practicing the spiritual disciplines of confession and meditation she has slowly come to embrace the idea that she is forgiven (1 Jn 1:9) and God has called her to "instruct" her boys (Eph 6:4). On the relational level God wants her to reclaim her authority and power to parent. A goal for the next conversation may be to reestablish her authority. Once this relational goal is achieved, she can move on to topic goals that directly address Dwayne's gaming and grades.

GWENN: I've done a lot of thinking lately about us and I'd like to say a couple of things. Would that be OK?

DWAYNE: I suppose.

GWENN: Your father and I messed up. Though we love each other, we couldn't keep it together. It all blew up. I really struggle with that. I sometimes think I'm a loser. More importantly, it hurt you and Miles and that keeps me up at night. It also caused me to pull back in parenting you. What right do I have to correct you? I've been doing a lot of soul-searching and praying. And I've concluded that I'm not a loser.

DWAYNE: Hey, I never said you were.

GWENN: Honey, I know you haven't. It's the funk I've been in. God knows I'm not perfect, but God has commanded me to parent you and your brother. In a perfect world, that would be with your father. But it isn't. Dwayne, before the Lord I am accountable to raise you in all areas. I care about you spiritually, personally and academically. While I often feel that I've screwed up my credibility with you, God has forgiven me and given me the authority to raise you. And that includes talking about your grades. I love you and I'm committed to

you. Let's both think about how to address your grades
without taking away your video gaming.

DWAYNE: What will that look like?

GWENN: (Laughing.) I'm not sure. But let's both of us think
about it. Deal?

DWAYNE: Do I have a choice?

GWENN: (Smiling.) What do you think?

Reestablishing her credibility will most likely be a long process
for Gwenn. It will require her to be rooted in daily meditation and
prayer that reminds her of her authority regardless of her boys'
fluctuating emotions or obedience. Just as her sons are commanded
to honor her regardless of her failures (Ex 20:12), she is to instruct
her children even if she doesn't do it perfectly or they don't respond.
Her sense of God-given authority will be increasingly evident to
Dwayne as they tackle topic goals focused on grades and video
games. Over time, Gwenn's content will be augmented, not diminished, by the relational progress she's made with Dwayne.

Epilogue

Over the years I lost track of the troubled couple armed with manila folders described in the introduction. I would periodically think of Vicki and Thomas and pray for restoration. A few years ago, I came across a person who had stayed in touch with them and was familiar with their struggles. Fearing the worst, I asked how they were doing. "They're hanging in there. Actually, they're doing better."

I was surprised and encouraged. "What's made the difference?" I asked.

"They're in counseling, attending a good church, and slowly learning to talk to each other."

Without oversimplifying their recovery, we can note two things this couple did that serve as an example to us we pursue healthy, productive communication with those we care about. They clung to the relationship and reopened lines of communication. In his classic book *The Miracle of Dialogue*, Reuel Howe gives insight into why these two factors are crucial:

> Dialogue is to love, what blood is to the body. When the flow of blood stops, the body dies. When dialogue stops, love dies and resentment and hate are born. But dialogue can restore a dead relationship. Indeed this is the miracle of dialogue: it can bring relationship into being, and it can bring into being once again a relationship that had died.[1]

When I met this troubled couple there was no life in their relationship. They were merely concerned with building a case
against each other while the dialogue between them gradually
ceased. The result? Resentment and hate were born and manila
folders began to be stuffed. Howe notes that for dialogue to heal,
individuals must "persist relentlessly."[2] While it's always an option
to dissolve a relationship, this book has focused on those we want
to save, not abandon.

Slowly, Vicki and Thomas found a way to talk *to* each other
rather than *at* each other. They are an example to all of us. If
properly used, our words can bring spiritual and physical healing
to those we care about as we speak truth and love. Author Eugene
Peterson graphically paraphrases one of the most powerful verses
on communication found in the Scriptures: "Words kill, words
give life; they're either poison or fruit—you choose" (Prov 18:21,
The Message).

As we enter difficult conversations with those we care about,
what will we offer them? Will it be poison or fruit?

Notes

INTRODUCTION

[1]Timothy Dudley-Smith, *Authentic Christianity: From the Writings of John Stott* (Downers Grove, IL: InterVarsity Press, 1995), p. 328.

CHAPTER 1

[1]To learn more visit: www.lovethatmax.com.

[2]Emanuella Grinberg, "Ending the R-Word: Ban It or Understand It?" CNN Living, CNN, March 7, 2012, www.cnn.com/2012/03/07/living/end-r-word.

[3]David A. Hubbard, *The Communicator's Commentary*, vol. 15, *Proverbs* (Dallas: Word, 1989), p. 399.

[4]Thank you to Scott Klingbeil for assembling and summarizing this research.

[5]"Key Facts," Newsroom, Facebook, 2013, newsroom.fb.com/key-facts.

[6]Twitter Engineering, "200 Million Tweets per Day," Blog, Twitter, June 30, 2011, blog.twitter.com/2011/200-million-tweets-day.

[7]"Statistics," YouTube, www.youtube.com/yt/press/statistics.html.

[8]Graeme McMillian, "How Big Is the Internet? (Spoiler: Not as Big as It'll Be in 2015)," *Time*, June 1, 2011, techland.time.com/2011/06/01/how-big-is-the-internet-spoiler-not-as-big-as-itll-be-in-2015/.

[9]Ibid.

[10]Deborah Tannen, *The Argument Culture: Moving from Debate to Dialogue* (New York: Random House, 1998), p. 14.

[11]The literary device of using "six . . . seven" suggests that this list, while specific, is not meant to be exhaustive. Derek Kidner, *Proverbs: An Introduction and Commentary* (Downers Grove, IL: InterVarsity Press, 1964), p. 73.

[12]In contrast to careless words are carefully scripted statements that strategically help present a particular image to another person. While not all scripted statements are inherently disingenuous, they can easily feed into

what theologian Alfred Plummer labels "calculated hypocrisy." This type of hypocrisy is evidenced by carefully crafted statements that present an image not matching personal convictions or behavior. See Alfred Plummer, *An Exegetical Commentary on the Gospel According to Saint Matthew*, 5th ed. (London: E. Stock, 1920), p. 181.

[13]Jeffery Hultin, *The Ethics of Obscene Speech in Early Christianity and Its Environment* (Boston: Brill, 2008), p. 67.

[14]Quoted in Barry D. Proner, "A Word About Words," *Journal of Analytical Psychology* 51 (2006): 423-35.

[15]Marilyn Chandler McEntyre, *Caring for Words in a Culture of Lies* (Grand Rapids: Eerdmans, 2009), p. 2.

[16]Zachary Estes and Sydney Felker, "Confidence Mediates the Sex Difference in Mental Rotation Performance," *Archives of Sexual Behavior* 41, vol. 3 (June 2012): 557-70.

[17]Caryl Stern-LaRosa and Ellen Hofheimer-Bettman, *Hate Hurts* (New York: Scholastic Paperbacks, 2000), p. 18.

[18]"One in Ten (12%) Parents Online, Around the World Say Their Child Has Been Cyberbullied, 24% Say They Know of a Child Who Has Experienced Same in Their Community," Ipsos, January 9, 2012, www.ipsos -na.com/news-polls/pressrelease.aspx?id=5462.

[19]Taken from: www.bullyingstatistics.org/content/cyber-bullying-statistics.html.

[20]Judith Butler, *Excitable Speech* (New York: Routledge, 1997), p. 1.

[21]Ronald Adler, Lawrence Rosenfeld and Russell Procotor II, *Interplay: The Process of Interpersonal Communication*, 12th ed. (New York: Oxford University Press, 2013), p. 66.

[22]I. A. Richards, "The Secret of 'Feedforward,'" *Saturday Review*, Feb. 3, 1968, p. 15.

[23]Rich Maloof, "A Town Swears Off Swearing," Daily Dose: Trends, Weird News, Analysis and More, MSN Living, June 12, 2012, living.msn.com /life-inspired/the-daily-dose-blog-post?post=fb3ad7b3-59af-4d6d-aab1 -acb63a38d580&gt1=.

CHAPTER 2

[1]R. M. Rezinik and Michael E. Roloff, "Getting off to a Bad Start: The Relationship Between Communication During an Initial Episode of a Serial Argument and Argument Frequency," *Communication Studies* 62 (2011): 291-306.

[2]W. J. Burk et al., "The Vicissitudes of Conflict Measurement: Stability and Reliability in the Frequency of Disagreements," *European Psychologist* 14 (2009): 153-59.

[3]Sam Vuchinich, "Starting and Stopping Spontaneous Family Conflicts," *Journal of Marriage and the Family* 49 (1987): 591-601.

[4]For a deeper look at communication climates, particularly applied to marriage, consider my book *Marriage Forecasting: Changing the Climate of Your Relationship One Conversation at a Time* (Downers Grove, IL: InterVarsity Press, 2010).

[5]Ronald Adler, Lawrence Rosenfeld and Russell Proctor, *Interplay: The Process of Interpersonal Communication*, 10th ed. (New York: Oxford University Press, 2007), p. 302.

[6]Ibid.

[7]See Amanda Doner Kagle, "Are We Lying to Ourselves About Deception?" *Social Service Review,* June 1998, pp. 234-44; J. Veroff, "Marital Commitment in the Early Years of Marriage," in W. Jones and J. Adams, eds., *Handbook of Interpersonal Commitment and Relationship Stability* (New York: Plenum, 1999), pp. 149-62.

[8]Julia Wood, *Interpersonal Communication: Everyday Encounters,* 6th ed. (Boston: Wadsworth, 2007), p. 198.

[9]For more, see *Speech Acts: An Essay in the Philosophy of Language* (London: Cambridge University Press, 1976).

[10]Adler et al., *Interplay*, p. 86.

[11]Albert Mehrabian, *Nonverbal Communication* (Chicago: Aldine-Atherton, 1972).

[12]This observation is not limited to interpersonal communication. Alan Schroeder, a Northeastern University professor who has written a book on the history of presidential debates, observes that the nonverbal cues candidates give off during a debate stay with us longer than their message. Did a candidate come across defensive? Was his message discredited by gestures that lacked confidence? Did his lack of eye contact with the audience suggest he's untrustworthy? While Schroeder focuses on politics, these are the very questions we ask in our conversations with others. For more information see Alan Schroeder, *Presidential Debates: Forty Years of High-Risk TV* (New York: Columbia University Press, 2001).

[13]C. S. Lewis, *The Screwtape Letters* (New York: Mentor, 1988), p. 11.

[14]Sandra Metts and William C. Cuptach, "Responses to Relational Trans-

gressions: Hurts, Anger, and Sometimes Forgiveness," in Brian H. Spirtzberg and William C. Cupach, eds., *The Dark Side of Interpersonal Communication*, 2nd ed. (Mahwah, NJ: Lawrence Erlbaum Associates, 2009), p. 219.

[15]Quoted in Julia T. Wood, "Introduction," in Julia T. Wood and Steve Duck, eds., *Composing Relationships: Communication in Everyday Life* (Belmont, CA: Wadsworth/Thompson, 2005), p. 6.

[16]Ibid, p. 8.

[17]Umberto Eco, *Travels in Hyperreality* (New York: Mariner, 1990), p. 164.

[18]Kathleen Perricone, "Heidi Klum Says She Wants to Be 'Friends' with Seal, Dishes on Relationship with Bodyguard," Yahoo!omg!, September 12, 2012, omg.yahoo.com/news/heidi-klum-says-she-wants-to-be -'friends'-with-seal--dishes-on-relationship-with-bodyguard.html.

CHAPTER 3

[1]Roger Fisher and Daniel Shapiro, *Beyond Reason: Using Emotions as You Negotiate* (New York: Penguin, 2005), p. 5.

[2]Ibid., p. 8.

[3]Jack Gibb, "Defensive Communication," *Journal of Communication* 11 (1961): 141-48.

[4]To read Gottman's criteria see John Gottman, *Seven Principles for Making Marriage Work* (New York: Crown, 1999), pp. 2-3.

[5]Philip Yancey, *Disappointment with God: Three Questions No One Asks Aloud* (Grand Rapids, MI: Zondervan, 1988), p. 52.

[6]G. Walter Hansen, "The Emotions of Jesus," *Christianity Today*, Feb. 3, 1977, p. 43.

[7]Julia T. Wood, *Interpersonal Communication: Everyday Encounters*, 6th ed. (Boston: Wadsworth, 2010), p. 175.

[8]Ibid., p. 177

[9]While as followers of Christ we can learn much from the perceptual view of emotions, it has at least one serious flaw—it seems to suggest that all of our emotional responses are socially constructed. If this is so, a person growing up in a racist community might feel pride in racist beliefs and actions. Are we merely at the mercy of our emotional communities in developing morality and appropriate emotions? The Scriptures tell us that God is not limited to what a particular community teaches about morality but has placed an awareness of his moral code in the hearts of

everyone (Rom 2:14). An awareness of God's moral code also produces certain emotions prompted by God's Spirit.

[10]Valeria Carofigio, Fiorella De Rosis and Roberto Grassano, "Dynamic Models of Multiple Emotions Activation," in Lola Cariamero and Ruth Aylett, eds., *Animating Expressive Characters for Social Interaction* (Amsterdam: John Benjamins, 2008), pp. 123-41.

[11]Ronald B. Adler, Lawrence B. Rosenfeld and Russell F. Proctor II, *Interplay: The Process of Interpersonal Communication*, 12th ed. (New York: Oxford University Press, 2013), p. 260.

[12]Chad M. Burton and Laura A. King, "Effects of (Very) Brief Writing on Health: The Two-Minute Miracle," *British Journal of Health Psychology* 00 (2007): 1-7.

[13]Fisher and Shapiro, *Beyond Reason*, p. 148.

[14]Daniel Goleman, *Social Intelligence: The New Science of Human Relationships* (New York: Random House, 2006), p. 115.

[15]Ellen S. Sullins, "Emotional Contagion Revisited: Effects of Social Comparison and Expressive Style on Mood Convergence," *Personality and Social Psychology Bulletin* 17 (1991): 166-74.

[16]Goleman, *Social Intelligence*, p. 16.

[17]Ibid.

[18]William Wilmot and Joyce Hocker, *Interpersonal Conflict*, 8th ed. (New York: McGraw Hill, 2011), p. 213.

CHAPTER 4

[1]NBC News staff, "American Eagle Flight Attendants' Argument Causes 4-Hour Delay at JFK," NBC News Travel, September 20, 2012, www .nbcnews.com/travel/american-eagle-flight-attendants-argument-causes -4-hour-delay-jfk-1B6000167.

[2]A. W. Tozer, *Tozer Speaks to Students*, ed. Lyle W. Dorsett (Camp Hill, PA: Wingspread, 1998), p. 9.

[3]Ibid.

[4]Thank you to my colleague David Nystrom for these insights.

[5]Donald S. Whitney, *Spiritual Disciplines for the Christian Life* (Colorado Springs, CO: NavPress, 1997), p. 21.

[6]Ibid., p. 17.

[7]Quoted in Bob Benson and Michael Benson, *Disciplines for the Inner Life* (Nashville: Thomas Nelson, 1989), p. 61.

[8]J. P. Moreland and Klaus Issler, *The Lost Virtue of Happiness: Discovering the Disciplines of the Good Life* (Colorado Springs, CO: NavPress, 2006), p. 46.

[9]Dallas Willard, *Spirit of the Disciplines* (San Francisco: Harper & Row, 1988), p. 3.

[10]Ibid., p. 5.

[11]"Superhero Movement Faces Its Own Kryptonite," *Orange County Register*, Oct. 18, 2011, News p. 10.

[12]Glenn T. Stanton, "The Christian Divorce Rate Myth (What You've Heard is Wrong)," Baptist Press, February 15, 2011, www.bpnews.net/BPnews .aSp?ID=34656.

[13]William Wilmot and Joyce Hocker, *Interpersonal Conflict*, 8th ed. (New York: McGraw Hill, 2011), p. 12

[14]Richard Foster, *Treasury of Christian Discipline* (New York: HarperCollins, 1996), p. 98.

[15]C. S. Lewis, *Mere Christianity* (New York: Macmillan, 1960), p. 168.

[16]Some may fear that a regular use of this prayer violates Jesus' warning that we should abstain from using meaningless repetitions in our prayer life (Mt 6:7). But theologian D. A. Carson notes that Jesus is not "forbidding all long prayers or all repetition. He Himself prayed at length (Lk. 6:12), repeated Himself in prayer (Mt. 26:44), and told a parable to show His disciples that 'they should always pray and not give up' (Lk. 6:12). His point is that His disciples should avoid meaningless, repetitive prayers offered under the misconception that mere length will make prayers efficacious." D. A. Carson, "Matthew," in *Expositor's Bible Commentary*, ed. Frank E. Gaebelein (Grand Rapids, MI: Zondervan, 1984), p. 166.

[17]Adele Ahlberg Calhoun, *Spiritual Disciplines Handbook: Practices That Transform Us* (Downers Grove, IL: InterVarsity Press, 2005), p. 92.

[18]Whitney, *Spiritual Disciplines*, p. 88.

[19]Quoted in John Blanchard, *Gathered Gold* (Welwyn, Hertfordshire, U.K.: Evangelical Press, 1984), p. 342.

[20]My colleague and IVP editor Al Hsu points out that every conversation entails three separate conversations that occur before, during and after: "the conversation we hope will take place, the one that actually happens, and the one we wish we had had." Personal correspondence, April 15, 2013.

[21]Thank you to Al Hsu for this powerful example.

[22]The Week's Editorial Staff, "Could 'awe therapy' make us nicer?" Yahoo! News, July 24, 2012, news.yahoo.com/could-awe-therapy-us-nicer-073100945.html.

[23]Calhoun, *Spiritual Disciplines Handbook*, p. 19.

CHAPTER 5

[1]M. Scott Peck, *The Road Less Traveled: A New Psychology of Love, Traditional Values, and Spiritual Growth* (New York: Simon and Schuster, 1978), p. 120.

[2]Eileen Wagner, "Listening: Hear Today, Probably Gone Tomorrow," *Business Journal,* May 11, 2001, p. 23.

[3]Judi Brownell and Andrew Wolvin, *What Every Student Needs to Know About Listening* (Upper Saddle River, NJ: Pearson, 2010), p. 100.

[4]John Gentile, "Telling the Untold Tales: Memory's Caretaker," *Text and Performance Quarterly* 24, no. 2 (2004): 201.

[5]David Isay, *Listening Is an Act of Love: A Celebration of American Life from the StoryCorps Project* (New York: Penguin, 2007). To listen to actual StoryCorps narratives see storycorps.org.

[6]Jimmie Manning, "Untold Stories," *Communication Monographs* 77, no. 4 (2010): 1.

[7]William Ury, *Getting Past No: Negotiations in Difficult Situations* (New York: Bantam Dell, 1993), p. 57.

[8]Judi Brownell, "Perceptions of Effective Listening: A Management Study," *Journal of Business Communication* 27 (1990): 401-15.

[9]C. S. Lewis, *An Experiment in Criticism* (Cambridge, U.K.: Cambridge University Press, 1961), p. 2.

[10]Ury, *Getting Past No,* p. 58.

[11]Julia Wood, *Interpersonal Communication: Everyday Encounters*, 6th ed. (Boston: Wadsworth, 2010), p. 154.

[12]William McKane, *Proverbs* (London: SCM, 1970), p. 507.

[13]Carl Trosset, "Obstacles to Open Discussion and Critical Thinking: The Grinnell College Study," *Change Magazine* 30 (1998): 44-49.

[14]Nicholas Carr, "Is Google Making Us Stupid? What the Internet Is Doing to Our Brains," *The Atlantic,* July/August, 2008, p. 58. Carr has expanded his essay into a thought-provoking book, *The Shallows: What the Internet Is Doing to Our Brains* (New York: W. W. Norton, 2010).

[15]McKane, *Proverbs,* p. 536.

[16]For more information on gender differences see the work of gender scholar Julia T. Wood in her excellent text *Gendered Lives*, 9th ed. (Boston: Wadsworth, 2011).

[17]Os Guinness, *Doubt* (Batavia, IL: Lion, 1976), p. 153.

[18]David Johnson, "Helpful Listening and Responding," in Kathleen M. Galvin, ed., *Making Connections: Readings in Relational Communication* (New York: Oxford University Press, 2011), p. 71.

[19]Sonia Johnson, *Going Out of Our Minds: The Metaphysics of Liberation* (Freedom, CA: Crossing, 1987), p. 132.

[20]Wood, *Interpersonal Communication*, p. 147.

[21]Vanessa Gregory, "Meditation Fit for a Marine: New Experiments with the Military Affirm the Benefits of Mindfulness," *Men's Journal*, November 2012, pp. 80-82.

[22]Michael Nyquist, "Learning to Listen," in *Ward Rounds* (Evanston, IL: Northwestern University Medical School, 1992), pp. 11-15.

CHAPTER 6

[1]"British Doctors Perform Heart Transplant Against Wishes of Girl," *The Coloradoan*, July 16, 1999, p. 3.

[2]Carol Gilligan, *In a Different Voice: Psychological Theory and Women's Development* (Cambridge, MA: Harvard University Press, 1982), p. xi.

[3]Christine M. Snapp and Mark R. Leary, "Hurt Feelings Among New Acquaintances: Moderating Effects of Interpersonal Familiarity," *Journal of Social and Personal Relationships* 18 (2001): 315-26.

[4]Charles Moore, *Provocations: Spiritual Writings of Kierkegaard* (Farmington, PA: Plough, 1999), p. xv.

[5]Julia Wood, *But I Thought You Meant . . . Misunderstandings in Human Communication* (Mountain View, CA: Mayfield, 1998), p. 43.

[6]Susan T. Fiske and Shelley E. Taylor, *Social Cognition* (New York: McGraw-Hill, 1991), p. 258.

[7]David Wann and Michael Schrader, "Controllability and Stability in the Self-serving Attributions of Sports Spectators," *Journal of Social Psychology* 140 (2000): 160-76.

[8]Jeff Goodell, "The Steve Jobs Nobody Knew: How an Insecure Hippie Kid Reinvented Himself—and Changed the World," *Rolling Stone*, October 27, 2011, p. 41.

[9]Elie Wiesel, *One Generation After* (New York: Avon, 1970), p. 11.

[10]Ronald Adler and George Rodman, *Understanding Human Communication*, 9th ed. (New York: Oxford University Press, 2006), p. 43.

[11]To read a summary of the study see Jamil Zaki, "What, Me Care? Young Are Less Empathetic," *Scientific American*, January 1, 2011, www.scientificamerican.com/article.cfm?id=what-me-care.

[12]Mar's observations are particularly relevant to my class exercise since *House of Sand and Fog* is an adaptation from the novel by Andre Dubus III.

[13]Henry Wadsworth Longfellow, *Outre-mer and Driftwood*, vol. 1 (London: Routledge and Sons, 1836), p. 405.

CHAPTER 7

[1]David Hubbard, *Proverbs* (Dallas, TX: Word Publishers, 1989), p. 50.

[2]Tim Downs, *Finding Common Ground* (Chicago: Moody Publishers, 1999), p. 100.

[3]Pauline Arrillaga, "The Mean Season: Why Is This Election's Campaign Advertising So Negative? Because It Works," *The Orange County Register*, Wednesday, Oct. 24, 2012, News p. 3.

[4]Philip Yancey, *Open Windows* (New York: Thomas Nelson, 1985), p. 182.

[5]Roger Fisher and William Ury, *Getting to Yes: Negotiating Agreement Without Giving In* (New York: Penguin, 1991), p. 24.

[6]Daniel Taylor, "Deconstructing the Gospel of Tolerance," *Christianity Today*, Jan. 11, 1999, p. 52.

[7]Ibid.

[8]Peter Elbow, *Embracing Contraries: Explorations in Learning and Teaching* (New York: Oxford University Press, 1986), p. 273.

[9]Peter Elbow, *Writing Without Teachers* (New York: Oxford University Press, 1998), p. 149.

[10]Elbow, *Embracing Contraries*, p. 273.

[11]Ibid.

[12]C. S. Lewis, *The Four Loves* (New York: Harcourt, Brace and Javanovich, 1960), p. 96.

[13]Peter Kreeft, *Making Sense of Suffering* (Ann Arbor, MI: Servant Books, 1986), p. 3.

[14]Larry Alex Taunton, "My Take: An Evangelical Remembers His Friend Hitchens," Belief Blog, CNN, December 16, 2011, religion.blogs.cnn.com/2011/12/16/my-take-an-evangelical-remembers-his-friend-hitchens/.

[15]J. Adrian Stanley, "Change of Focus: As the 'River of Culture' Rages On,

Jim Daley Will Stay Rooted—but Respectful," *The Independent*, June 9-15, 2011, p. 17.

[16]Ibid.

[17]Richard Dawkins, "Why I Want All Our Children to Read the King James Bible," *The Guardian*, May 19, 2012, www.theguardian.com/science/2012/may/19/richard-dawkins-king-james-bible/print.

[18]Hubbard, *Proverbs*, p. 274.

[19]The only way the elders could help resolve the issue was if both disagreeing parties recognized that they belonged to the same community and the authority of the elders. Today, Americans are so fractured and isolated within differing ideological camps that there is no longer a sense of commonality as citizens committed to a common goal such as democracy or patriotism. In such a fractured climate, who can serve as respected elders who can adjudicate disagreements?

[20]Over the years some parents have been concerned that a Christian professor would have students question the authenticity of the Bible. What if they were to conclude that it wasn't trustworthy and were tempted, like Mark, to walk away from the faith? I do not take such concerns lightly. If the mere asking of a question will cause a student to walk away from the faith, then it is better that it happen while at a Christian university where he or she can get answers and deal with doubts. Simply ignoring or suppressing questions and doubts will force a student to turn off his or her mind and embrace an anti-intellectual approach to faith. In the long run, ignoring doubts or avoiding asking questions will inhibit the growth of an enduring faith.

[21]For the rest of the questions see Peter Kreeft and Ronald K. Tacelli, *Handbook of Christian Apologetics* (Downers Grove, IL: InterVarsity Press, 1994).

CHAPTER 8

[1]Robert Cialdini, *Influence: The Psychology of Persuasion* (New York: William Morrow, 1984), p. 17.

[2]Richard Leakey and Roger Lewin, *People of the Lake: Mankind and its Beginnings* (New York: Anchor, 1978), p. 78.

[3]Cialdini, *Influence*, p. 19.

[4]Ibid., p. 20.

[5]Dennis Regan, "Effects of a Favor and Liking on Compliance," *Journal of Experimental Social Psychology* 7 (1971): 627-39.

[6]Jennifer Kunz, "Social Status Difference in Response to Christmas Cards," *Perceptual and Motor Skills* 90 (2000): 573-76.

[7]Her study is complicated by the fact that half the cards were sent to strangers with the sender simply being a person's first name. Receiving a card from a low-status person resulted in few responding (less than one-tenth). It seems that the rule of reciprocation can be weakened or heightened based on our perception of the value of the person doing the actions.

[8]Irenaus Eibl-Eibesfeldt, *Ethology: The Biology of Behavior* (New York: Holt, Rinehart and Winston, 1975), pp. 55-57.

[9]The principle of reaping and sowing is not limited to the book of Galatians. The theme can be traced throughout Scripture: Job 4:8; 31:8; Ps 126:5; Prov 11:21; 22:8; Jer 12:13; Mic 6:15; Mt 6:26; 25:24, 26; Lk 19:21; Jn 4:36-37; Rev 14:15-16.

[10]John Stott, *The Message of Galatians* (Downers Grove, IL: InterVarsity Press, 1968), p. 166.

[11]Ibid., p. 165.

[12]Cornelius Plantinga Jr., *Not the Way It's Supposed to Be: A Breviary of Sin* (Grand Rapids, MI: Eerdmans, 1995), p. 65.

[13]Cialdini, *Influence*, p. 43.

[14]Quoted in Stott, *Galatians*, p. 172.

[15]"Controversy Emerges Over Obama's Choice of Inauguration Pastor," PBS NewsHour, December 18, 2008, www.pbs.org/newshour/bb/religion/july-dec08/rickwarren_12-18.html.

CHAPTER 9

[1]Eugene Peterson, *Subversive Spirituality* (Grand Rapids, MI: Eerdmans, 1997), p. 189.

[2]Ibid.

[3]Em Griffin, *A First Look at Communication Theory*, 6th ed. (Boston: McGraw Hill, 2006), p. 193.

[4]George Herbert Mead, *Mind, Self, and Society* (Chicago: University of Chicago Press, 1934).

[5]To read the entire study see Ruth Ann Clark and Jesse Delia, "Cognitive Complexity, Social Perspective-Taking, and Functional Persuasive Skills in Second-to-Ninth-Grade Students," *Human Communication Research* 3 (1977): 128-34.

[6]Walter Fisher and W. Ury, *Getting to Yes: Negotiating Agreement Without Giving In* (New York: Penguin, 1981), p. 48.

[7]"Physicians Conceded They've Misled Patients," *Orange County Register*, February 9, 2012, News p. 7.

[8]Gregg Ten Elshof, *I Told Me So: Self-Deception and the Christian Life* (Grand Rapids, MI: Eerdmans, 2009), p. 130.

[9]George Santayana, *The Life of Reason: Reason in Common Sense* (New York: Dover, 1980), p. 190.

[10]William Wilmot and Joyce Hocker, *Interpersonal Conflict*, 8th ed. (New York: McGraw Hill, 2011), p. 72.

[11]B. R. Brown, "Face-Saving and Face-Restoration in Negotiation," in *Negotiations*, ed. D. Druckman (Beverly Hills, CA: Sage, 1977), p. 175.

[12]Wilmot and Hocker, *Interpersonal Conflict*, p. 76.

[13]Ibid, p. 73.

[14]Ibid, p. 77.

[15]Michael Glerup, *Gregory of Nyssa: Sermons on the Beatitudes* (Downers Grove, IL: InterVarsity Press, 2012), p. 41.

CHAPTER 10

[1]Adele Ahlberg Calhoun, *Spiritual Disciplines Handbook: Practices That Transform Us* (Downers Grove, IL: InterVarsity Press, 2005), p. 92.

[2]Aman El-Alayli et al., "I Don't Mean to Sound Arrogant, but . . . The Effects of Using Disclaimers on Person Perception," *Personality and Social Psychology Bulletin* 34 (2008): 130-43.

[3]Daniel J. Canary, "Managing Interpersonal Conflict: A Model of Events Related to Strategic Choices," in *Handbook of Communication and Social Interaction Skills*, ed. John Green and Brant Burleson (Mahwah, NJ: Erlbaum, 2003), pp. 515-49.

CHAPTER 11

[1]"Penn Jillette Gets a Gift of a Bible," YouTube, August 4, 2009, www.youtube.com/watch?v=ZhG-tkQ_Q2w.

[2]There is no concept of original sin in Islam. While Muslims believe that Adam and Eve did sin, they eventually repented and asked Allah for forgiveness. "Then Adam learned form his Lord certain words, and Allah accepted his repentance for He is oft-forgiving, Most Merciful" (Quran 2:37). However, while humans are not born into sin, the Quran says we

still need rules from Allah to counteract our ignorance or disobedience. [3]"The balance that day will be true (to a nicety): those whose scale (of good) will be heavy, will prosper. Those whose scales will be light, will find their souls in perdition, for that they wrongly treated Our Signs" (Quran 7:8-9). [4]B. Ghosh, "In America's Most Muslim City, Fears of a Backlash," *Time*, November 30, 2009, p. 6. [5]There are three acceptable ways to destroy a damaged Quran. First, one must wrap it in cloth and bury it in a sentimental location. Second, one may burn it so long as it is burned by itself in a clean container. The recent uproar in Afghanistan over American troops burning Qurans is because they accidently burned them along with trash. Third, a Quran may be shredded so long as every page is individually shredded.

CHAPTER 12

[1]Douglas Gentile and David Walsh, *A Normative Study of Family Media Habits* (Minneapolis: National Institute on Media and the Family, 2002). [2]D. A. Gentile et al., "The Effects of Violent Video Game Habits on Adolescent Hostility, Aggressive Behaviors, and School Performance," *Journal of Adolescence* 27 (2004): 5-22. [3]For more on how men are socialized into a masculine community, see this classic work: James Doyle, *The Male Experience*, 3rd ed. (Dubuque, IA: Brown and Benchmark, 1997). [4]William Wilmot and Joyce Hocker, *Interpersonal Conflict*, 8th ed. (New York: McGraw Hill, 2011), p. 77.

EPILOGUE

[1]Reuel Howe, *The Miracle of Dialogue* (New York: Seabury, 1963), p. 3. [2]Ibid.

Name and Subject Index

Scripture Index

Also by Tim Muehlhoff

The God Conversation
*Using Stories and Illustrations
to Explain Your Faith*

Authentic Communication
*Christian Speech
Engaging Culture*

Marriage Forecasting
*Changing the Climate of Your
Relationship One Conversation
at a Time*

www.timmuehlhoff.com